THE PLOUGHSHARES
POETRY READER

THE PLOUGHSHARES
POETRY READER

Edited and with an introduction by
Joyce Peseroff

Ploughshares Books
Watertown
1986

Library of Congress Card Number: 86-06319
ISBN 0-933277-02-4

First printing, January 1987

Manufactured in The United States of America

This book is dedicated to the
Ploughshares poetry editors:

Frank Bidart
Rosellen Brown
William Corbett
Lorrie Goldensohn
David Gullette
Donald Hall
Paul Hannigan
Stratis Haviaras
Seamus Heaney
Fanny Howe
Thomas Lux
Gail Mazur
Robert Pinsky
James Randall
Lloyd Schwartz
Jane Shore
George Starbuck
Richard Tillinghast
Ellen Bryant Voigt
Alan Williamson

and to the memory of
Elizabeth Bishop, friend to
some and mentor to many
associated with the magazine.

Acknowledgements

"I am tired of being the child, the maiden aunt," reprinted from I'M NOT YOUR LAUGHING DAUGHTER, by Ellen Bass (Amherst: University of Massachusetts Press, 1973), copyright © 1973 by The University of Massachusetts Press.

"The Sacrifice," from THE SACRIFICE, copyright © 1983 by Frank Bidart. Reprinted with permission of Random House, Inc.

"Ellen West," from THE BOOK OF THE BODY, copyright © 1977 by Frank Bidart. Reprinted by permission of Farrar, Straus and Giroux, Inc.

"The Attache Case," from IN A SURF OF STRANGERS. Copyright © 1981 by George Bogin. Reprinted with permission of University Presses of Florida.

"Sorting It Out," from RELATIONS by Philip Booth. Copyright © 1979 by Philip Booth. Reprinted by permission of Viking Penguin, Inc.

"The Hammer Falls, Is Falling," copyright © 1985 by Marianne Boruch. Reprinted from VIEW FROM THE GAZEBO by permission of Wesleyan University Press.

"Big Sheep Knocks You About," copyright © 1983 by Sharon Bryan. Reprinted from SALT AIR by permission of Wesleyan University Press.

"Star for a Glass," from THE FIRES THEY KEEP, copyright © 1986 by Michael Burkard. Reprinted with permission of Metro Books.

"Hometown," from SONGS OF JUBILEE. $8.00 Copyright © 1986 by Sam Cornish. Reprinted with permission of Unicorn Press, P.O. Box 3307, Greensboro, NC 27402.

"Versions," "Age," Robert Creeley, MIRRORS, copyright © 1983 by Robert Creeley. Reprinted by permission of New Directions Publishing Corporation.

"New England Interlude," from MAGPIE ON THE GALLOWS, copyright © 1982 by Madeline DeFrees. Reprinted with permission of Copper Canyon Press.

"Spider Web," from CEMETERY NIGHTS, copyright © 1987 by Stephen Dobyns. Reprinted by permission of Viking Penguin, Inc.

"That Time, That Country," from EVE NAMES THE ANIMALS. Copyright © 1985 by Susan Donnelly. Reprinted with the permission of Northeastern University Press.

"Taking In Wash," by Rita Dove. Reprinted from THOMAS AND BEULAH by permission of Carnegie-Mellon University Press. Copyright © 1986 by Rita Dove.

"On the Eating of Mice" and "Feeding the Dog," originally "The Melting," Copyright © 1985 by Russell Edson. Reprinted from THE WOUNDED BREAKFAST by permission of Wesleyan University Press.

"At the Bus Stop; Eurydice," "Ellery Street," and "Rereading Old Writing," from STRANGERS. Copyright © 1983 by David Ferry. Reprinted with permission of The University of Chicago Press.

"My Father's Store," from WINDOWS FACING EAST. Copyright © 1986 by Caroline Finkelstein. Reprinted with permission of Dragon Gate Press.

"From Our Mary To Me," from DANCE SCRIPT FOR ELECTRIC BALLERINA. Copyright © 1983 by Alice Fulton. Reprinted with permission of University of Pennsylvania Press.

"Letter to a Daughter," from THE TETHER. Copyright © 1982 by Lorrie Goldensohn. Reprinted with permission of L'Epervier Press.

"I Was Taught Three," from Jorie Graham, HYBRIDS OF PLANTS AND OF GHOSTS (Princeton Series of Contemporary Poets). Copyright © 1980 by Princeton University Press. Reprinted with permission of Princeton University Press.

"Kimono," from Jorie Graham, EROSION (Princeton Series of Contemporary Poets). Copyright © 1983 by Princeton University Press. Reprinted with permission of Princeton University Press.

"The Department," "The Thrush Relinquished," Allen Grossman, THE WOMAN ON THE BRIDGE OVER THE CHICAGO RIVER. Copyright © 1979 by Allen Grossman. Reprinted with permission of New Directions Publishing Corporation.

"The Henyard Round," from THE HAPPY MAN. Copyright © 1986 by Donald Hall. Reprinted with permission of Random House, Inc.

"Mother-land'scape (Letters)," from ONE LONG POEM, copyright © 1982 by William Harmon. Reprinted with permission from Louisiana State University Press.

Contents

Joyce Peseroff

Introduction

The Ploughshares Poetry Reader began taking form five years ago, when I was still the magazine's managing editor. I spent several days a week in the Watertown office reading, reviewing, and culling, excited by the daily mail's quota of poems, while exchanging literary judgment — and gossip — with our editors and directors, and continuing, informally, the ongoing dialogue which has been *Ploughshares'* concern since its inception over fifteen years ago. With its policy of rotating editorship, and a new editorial point of view introduced in each issue, *Ploughshares* has, over eleven volumes published since 1971, maintained debate on a question which has been at the center of the lively, pluralist tradition of American poetry — what makes a good poem?

If the past twenty years have brought a new renaissance in American letters, diversity has helped to shape it. It is perhaps the template of our literature, split at the root from the beginning, with some writers turning outward for models, and others to the continent's leafy interior. If modern traditions in American poetry begin with the impossible marriage of Walt Whitman and Emily Dickinson, then it is not surprising that there is today no single answer, no one center, no dominant style, clique, movement, or mode. When *Ploughshares* began as an outlet for the work of a group of Iowa Writers' Workshop veterans, New York School aficionadoes, Harvard University graduate assistants, and Black Mountain descendants — all meeting in a Dubliner's Cambridge bar, from which the new quarterly took its name — it provided a needed forum in which writers themselves could define what constitutes good writing. Though many magazines arise in order to broadcast a new movement, explore a linguistic philosophy, and actively lobby for an aesthetic or regional supremacy (*The Fugitive, Black Mountain Review,* Robert Bly's *The Fifties, Sixties,* and *Seventies,* Cid Corman's *Origin,* and the feminist *Thirteenth Moon* all come to mind), *Ploughshares* has always attempted the opposite—taking poetry out of these individual sanctuaries, inviting poets to share common ground, and allowing the reader to judge what is valuable and vital within each style. Our aim has been to open our readers' eyes with unexpected news.

As I worked with editors like Seamus Heaney, Gail Mazur, Lorrie Goldensohn, Donald Hall, and Jane Shore, I witnessed the writerly passion of each transformed into a collection that spoke for a certain set of literary values. Through the process of shaping an issue, each coordinating editor created what director DeWitt Henry has called "a context of appreciation" for individual writers. This is the texture I have attempted to reproduce, the values I have tried to reflect, and a diversity I feel called to celebrate, in *The Ploughshares Poetry Reader,* offering the best of a generation's talent represented by those poems which are the emerging classics of our time.

What are the qualities which have animated our poetry since the 1970's, and which I have tried to reflect? They involve content and style; the use of metaphor to subvert cultural and aesthetic expectation:

> A head of cheese raised by wolves
> or mushrooms
> recently rolled into
> the village, it
> could neither talk nor
> walk upright.
>
> (James Tate, "The Wild Cheese")

as well as the deliberate avoidance of arresting images:

> He thinks he'll hate it
> and when he does die
> at last, he supposes
> he still won't know it.
>
> (Robert Creeley, "Age")

They include the emergence of a vulnerable, cultivated, slightly ironical "I":

> Although I am taking courses in the language
> of children, penguin socialization
> and creative writing, now, in my dotage —
>
> dotage, what a striking word — I find
> myself betrayed — betrayed — by what?
> Betrayed! That's what it means to be human.
>
> (Phyllis Janowitz, "Although I
> Am Taking Courses in the Language")

as well as a desire for impersonality sought in hermetic symbolism:

> Cistercians, all 'sister,' in any case
> sexless, insist
> the last & best
> is left for X.
>
> (Fanny Howe, "Onlie X")

Language may be taut and dense, as in the work of Charles Wright and Eleanor Ross Taylor, or relaxed, colloquial, and plain as it is in poems by Mark Halliday and Ellen Bass. The question of the line and how to break it — or whether to dispense with it altogether, as in the journal entries of Joe Brainard or the prose poems of Russell Edson — remains even as a tide of formalism returns to the extensive, irregular shore of free verse.

The great driven careers of the past — Plath, Berryman, Jarrell, and Lowell — together with great mythmakers like Jeffers and Olson, have been replaced, more and more, by poets of the microcosm, of the cherished intimate, and of the domestic, as the influence of two world wars recedes and history is dominated by personal history. The methods of these poets and their focus on childhood may derive from Freud but go back to Wordsworth, perhaps the first to write whole poems in the manner of meandering, meditative digression:

> Who has not watched the ocean at night
> and heard its old invitation?
> That same dusky word licks through the pines.

> I press my face against the screen
> and remember I did this exact thing
> as a child on my grandmother's farm . . .
>
> (Michael Ryan, "Why")

Yet if a rift exists between poets with broad historical interests — like Anthony Hecht or Frank Bidart — and those who create drama within a private world — like Linda Pastan or Carol Muske — it is bridged by others like Seamus Heaney, whose own backyard is a minefield, and by Robert Pinsky, whose figured wheel rolls past and present into one ball.

Other concerns in this anthology include an interest in the long poem, represented by Frank Bidart's "Ellen West," Richard Hugo's "1805 Gratiot," Lloyd Schwartz's "Who's On First," and Mona Van Duyn's "Letters to a Father," as well as excerpts from book-length poems by William Harmon and James McMichael. This interest may be allied to a return to trust in narrative, once ceded by poetry to fiction and, in the 1970's, ceded by fiction to film, and now found in the work of writers as different from one another as Thomas Lux and Alice Mattison, Donald Hall and Richard Howard. But for every poet who writes out of a sense of location, a personal history, a coherent and concrete set of external circumstances and primary anecdotes:

> All day we travel from bed to bed, our children
> clutching home-made bouquets
> of tulips and jonquils, hyacinth,
> handfuls of yellow salad from the fields.
> In Pittsylvania County, our dead face east,
> my great-grandfather and his sons facing
> what is now a stranger's farm.
>
> (Ellen Bryant Voigt, "Visiting the Graves")

there is another who aims to bleach all cultural and personal pattern from the fabric of experience, attempting a pure art:

> Now, during a full moon, the pond fills with animals
> waiting for death. They call their pleasure
> the other side of the silver coin.
>
> (Trish Reeves, "The Silver Coin")

Yet the preoccupations of poets are said to be changeless: love and death, parents and children, sickness and old age; imprisonment, dispossession, and exile, both internal and external, as in poems by Sam Cornish and Bill Knott; public political passion and fear of ultimate war, evident in work by Maxine Kumin and Denise Levertov; memory, grief, desire, and joy; estrangement of spirit from flesh, body from mind, and God from the world; metaphorical visions of reality found in poems by Charles Simic and Allen Grossman, as well as Jane Kenyon's or Richard Tillinghast's songs to a loved, particular place. Ultimately, of course, language is the poet's true subject, and each poet in *The Ploughshares Poetry Reader* makes a different claim on it, shaping a voice through which the mute world might speak.

The selection process for this anthology began five years ago with my enthusiasm for a number of writers whose work I had followed through the pages of the magazine — Frank Bidart, William Corbett, David Ferry, Allen Grossman, Paul Hannigan, Phyllis Janowitz, Jane Kenyon, Bill Knott, Thomas Lux, Alice Mattison, Gail Mazur, Robert Pinsky, Lloyd Schwartz, Maura Stanton, Eleanor Ross Taylor, and Ellen Bryant Voigt, among others. I felt that together they made a statement about the direction American poetry would take in the final decades of this century. When plans for the book proceeded, and I found my forum a reality, I returned to back issues of the magazine, noting and adding those writers whose work I respected and whose poems appeared consistently throughout several volumes, including Madeline DeFrees, Fanny Howe, David Ignatow, Maxine Kumin, James McMichael, James Merrill, Carole Oles, Michael Ryan, Jane Shore, Charles Simic, and James Tate. These, together with the editors who coordinated each issue, comprise the "Ploughshares" poets; they form the backbone of this book.

Yet reading and rereading eleven volumes, I could not help but find poems that kept their "freshness as a metal keeps its fragrance," as Robert Frost said about all good poems. I added each one to my growing list of work that belonged in such a collection; soon I had hundreds of titles by almost two hundred poets. Then came the difficult task of reducing this list to fit a format that could not exceed a limited number of pages and a limited publications budget; this was the real work of editing.

I decided, early on, that I would include only those poems written in English (including work by Irish writers Seamus Heaney, Derek Mahon, and Paul Muldoon). A second anthology could be drawn from *Ploughshares'* list of poetry in translation, which includes a "first" publication of Montale's long poem, "Xenia," Elizabeth Bishop's translations of Carlos Drummond de Andrade, and Stratis Haviaras' international writing issue.

It also became necessary to limit each contributor to a maximum of three poems. Rarely, we could not obtain permission from a publisher to reprint material which had appeared in a book since its publication in *Ploughshares*. And although by the time this anthology appears at least two more poetry issues will be complete and ready for distribution, I have had to limit my selections to *Ploughshares'* first eleven volumes. To those who wish to hear more of the magazine's "ongoing debate," I suggest a subscription ($15 / yr. to Ploughshares, Box 529, Cambridge, Mass. 02139).

Within these limitations, I have tried to balance matter and manner to reveal accurately the magazine's cosmopolitan focus. I have also tried to represent *Ploughshares'* tradition of discovery (almost half of the poets included here contributed work to the magazine before they had placed a manuscript—Jorie Graham, Brad Leithauser, Robert Pinsky, Katha Pollitt, among others) by placing writers who have not yet published a book together with acknowledged masters, and those in midcareer who will be celebrated as their peers.

I could not, and did not, accomplish this task alone. My judgment was augmented, and my prejudices challenged, by those coordinating editors whose comments and consultations helped me to alter and improve the manuscript in progress: Frank Bidart, William Corbett, Lorrie Goldensohn, Donald

Hall, Seamus Heaney, Thomas Lux, Gail Mazur, James Randall, Lloyd Schwartz, and Jane Shore. I would like to thank over a dozen publishers for their generous cooperation, and all the authors for their prompt response to our forms and queries. Thanks also to those who assisted me in the myriad details of typing, collating, and correspondence: Michelle Fredette, Ann Greenberger, Don Lee, and Jennifer Rose.

The support I received from Ploughshares directors DeWitt Henry and Peter O'Malley made this anthology a reality. I am grateful for the opportunity they have offered, and the unstinting help they have given, over the five years it has taken for the plough to break ground and the seed to bear fruit.

Thanks, also, to the Massachusetts Council on the Arts and Humanities, the National Endowment for the Arts, the Coordinating Council of Literary Magazines, Emerson College, and to our patrons and readers for their continuing support.

Joyce Peseroff
November 1986

Steve Albert

City Lights: I Took That Picture

I stood in front of City Lights
the other afternoon.
Allen Ginsberg had just dropped
off a manuscript called "Howl."
Lawrence let me read it.
I thought it was quite good.
Bob Kaufman tried to punch me,
but I don't think he particularly
disliked the manuscript.
Jack Kerouac and Neal Cassady
drove up. Neal was not driving
100 miles per hour down Columbus,
but he did park in the bus zone.
I think that Neal was living in
San Jose and Jack was
staying down on Fifth Street.
Kenneth Rexroth offered me
a cigarette and said he
would introduce me to Neal.
(Jack and I had been good
friends since Denver.)
I thought Neal a particularly
pleasant person.
Bob Kaufman tried to punch me,
but I don't think he particularly
disliked Neal.
Jack let me read his manuscript.
I think it was called "On the Road."
I thought it was quite good.

Bob Kaufman tried to punch me
but I don't think he particularly
disliked the manuscript.
They all went downstairs
to read at one of the big round tables.
I stayed on the sidewalk to talk
with Richard Brautigan. He had been
writing in the reading room of the Presidio
branch library out on Sacramento.
I recommended he try to publish
his manuscript— "You might want
to call it 'The Abortion,'" I suggested.
Bob Kaufman tried to punch us both
but I don't think he particularly
disliked us.
Gary Snyder joined me almost immediately
after Richard went inside. We discussed
various koans and practiced clapping
with one hand. Bob Kaufman
was rather confused.
Lawrence yelled from inside that
he wanted everybody out. I suppose
no one was buying Whitman
or the Cantos. Everyone stood in
front of the store while I took
their picture. You may have seen
this picture. I am not in the picture,
but I am the one who took it.
It was also my camera.
All of this is true and happened
in front of City Lights. Bob Kaufman
will confirm this.

Ellen Bass

Untitled

I am tired of being the child, the maiden aunt,
the Poor Miss Bass who never had any chemistry,
back with all those freshmen, too old and unprepared.
I'm tired of sitting through the sports festival
watching the cheerleaders, accurate and graceless,
the girls with fat knees,
the boys straining, lips pulled inward, eyes small pig-like slits.
I'm tired of saving theatre programs, writing in my diary,
drinking ginger ale, dreaming of underpants slit at the crotch
like the ones in the uptown boardwalk windows.

I'm tired of masturbating
and not masturbating,
tired of scaring men away when I stand up or laugh.
My opened palm is a fan of green leaves,
my fingers, brown and glossy, polished wood,
but they are not enough.

After the basketball game, when Takio and I sit in the back
        seat,
his shoulder touches mine as we go around a curve
and there is a surge in my cunt, in my lungs, through my
        bowels.
Then, a second wave, of
almost repulsion, telling me how closed I have become.
Like the windows of the air conditioned trains,
like cellophane around a candy box,
like the seal of a whiskey bottle or of a letter,

I am insulated.
I am a Catholic school girl.
I am a widowed woman.

An old man blows me kisses on the street.
A child gives me sweet azuki bean cakes.
Then I ride on the bus next to a fraternity boy from Texas.
Like the night we stopped in North Carolina,
I was still half asleep, went into the diner, toward the
        bathroom.
Some men in a booth just laughing at me, in my hiking boots,
my frizzy hair, my glasses.
I knew I was beautiful, so I just smiled.
But here I don't know it;
there's nothing to remind me.
Only lovely Japanese women, shy and promising,
ready to undo their summer kimono for the Texas boys.

I've had enough of this.
I want Boston
where the men don't check their watches
and I can let my nipples show through colored t-shirts.
I want Boston where I scream and laugh and yodel,
where I pay electric bills, drive a car, unlock the door to my
        apartment.
Boston, where I stay in contact with my heart and my cunt,
my ass not just for shitting, my legs for more than
        transportation,
where more than one man wants to fuck and read my stories,
eating yogurt, calling information for the weather in Maine.

I've had it.
Call the airport.
Get the luggage. Wire Western Union.
Give my regards to Broadway.
Draco the Snako is splitting from here.

Frank Bidart

Ellen West

I love sweets,—
                    heaven
would be dying on a bed of vanilla ice cream . . .

But my true self
is thin, all profile

and effortless gestures, the sort of blond
elegant girl whose
                    body is the image of her soul.

—My doctors tell me I must give up
this ideal;
            but I
WILL NOT . . . cannot.

Only to my husband I'm not simply a "case."

But he is a fool. He married
meat, and thought it was a wife.

●   ●   ●

Why am I a girl?

I ask my doctors, and they tell me they
don't know, that it is just "given."

But it has such
implications—;
                    and sometimes,
I even feel like a girl.

         •   •   •

Now, at the beginning of Ellen's thirty-second year, her
physical condition has deteriorated still further. Her use
of laxatives increases beyond measure. Every evening she
takes sixty to seventy tablets of a laxative, with the result
that she suffers tortured vomiting at night and violent
diarrhea by day, often accompanied by a weakness of the
heart. She has thinned down to a skeleton, and weighs
only 92 pounds.

         •   •   •

About five years ago, I was in a restaurant,
eating alone
                    with a book. I was
not married, and often did that . . .

—I'd turn down
dinner invitations, so I could eat alone;

I'd allow myself two pieces of bread, with
butter, at the beginning, and three scoops of
vanilla ice cream, at the end,—

                                        sitting there alone
with a book, both in the book
and out of it, waited on, idly
watching people,—

when an attractive young man
and woman, both elegantly dressed,
sat next to me.
                    She was beautiful—;

with sharp, clear features, a good
bone structure—;
                    if she took her make-up off
in front of you, rubbing cold cream
again and again across her skin, she still would be
beautiful—
            more beautiful.

And he,—
            I couldn't remember when I had seen a man
so attractive. I didn't know why. He was almost

a male version
            of her,—

I had the sudden, mad notion that I
wanted to be his lover . . .

—Were they married?
                    were *they* lovers?

They didn't wear wedding rings.

Their behavior was circumspect. They discussed
politics. They didn't touch . . .

—How could I discover?

                    Then, when the first course
arrived, I noticed the way

each held his fork out for the other

to taste what he had ordered . . .

                                      They did this
again and again, with pleased looks, indulgent
smiles, for each course,
                         more than once for *each* dish—;
much too much for just friends . . .

—Their behavior somehow sickened me;

the way each *gladly*
put the *food* the other had offered *into his mouth*—;

I knew what they were. I knew they slept together.

An immense depression came over me . . .

—I knew I could never
with such ease allow another to put food into my mouth:

happily *myself* put food into another's mouth—;

I knew that to become a wife I would have to give up my
                ideal.

                    •   •   •

Even as a child,
I saw that the "natural" process of aging

is for one's middle to thicken—
one's skin to blotch;

as happened to my mother.
And her mother.
>   *I loathed "Nature."*

At twelve, pancakes
became the most terrible thought there is . . .

I shall *defeat* "Nature."

In the hospital, when they
weigh me, I wear weights secretly sewn into my belt.

•   •   •

January 16. The patient is allowed to eat in her room, but
comes readily with her husband to afternoon coffee. Pre-
viously she had stoutly resisted this on the ground that
she did not really eat but devoured like a wild animal.
This she demonstrated with utmost realism . . . . Her
physical examination showed nothing striking. Salivary
glands are markedly enlarged on both sides.
    January 21. Has been reading *Faust* again. In her
diary, writes that art is the "mutual permeation" of the
"world of the body" and the "world of the spirit." Says
that her own poems are "hospital poems . . . weak—
without skill or perseverance; only managing to beat their
wings softly."
    February 8. Agitation, quickly subsided again. Has
attached herself to an elegant, very thin female patient.
Homo-erotic component strikingly evident.
    February 15. Vexation, and torment. Says that her
mind forces her always to think of eating. Feels herself
degraded by this. Has entirely, for the first time in years,
stopped writing poetry.

•   •   •

Callas is my favorite singer, but I've only
seen her once—;

I've never forgotten that night . . .

—It was in *Tosca,* she had long before
lost weight, her voice
had been, for years,
                    deteriorating, half itself . . .

When her career began, of course, she was fat,

enormous—; in the early photographs,
sometimes I almost don't recognize her . . .

The voice too then was enormous—

healthy; robust; subtle; but capable of
crude effects, even vulgar,
                    almost out of
high spirits, too much health . . .

But soon she felt that she must lose weight,—
that all she was trying to express

was obliterated by her body,
buried in flesh—;
                    abruptly, within
four months, she lost at least sixty pounds . . .

—The gossip in Milan was that Callas
had swallowed a tapeworm.

But of course she hadn't.

                    The *tapeworm*
was her *soul* . . .

—How her soul, uncompromising,
insatiable,
        must have loved eating the flesh from her bones,

revealing this extraordinarily
mercurial; fragile; masterly creature . . .

—But irresistibly, nothing
stopped there; the huge voice

also began to change: at first, it simply diminished
in volume, in size,
        then the top notes became
shrill, unreliable—at last,
usually not there at all . . .

—No one knows *why.* Perhaps her mind,
ravenous, still insatiable, sensed

that to struggle with the *shreds* of a voice

must make her artistry subtler, more refined,
more capable of expressing humiliation,
rage, betrayal . . .

—Perhaps the opposite. Perhaps her spirit
loathed the unending struggle

to *embody* itself, to *manifest* itself, on a stage whose

mechanics, and suffocating customs,
seemed expressly designed to annihilate spirit . . .

—I know that in *Tosca,* in the second act,
when, humiliated, hounded by Scarpia,
she sang *Vissi d'arte*
        —"I lived for art"—

and in torment, bewilderment, at the end she asks,
with a voice reaching
                          harrowingly for the notes,

"Art has *repaid* me LIKE THIS?"

                                        I felt I was watching
autobiography—
                    an art; skill;
virtuosity

miles distant from the usual soprano's
athleticism,—
                    the usual musician's dream
of virtuosity *without* content . . .

—I wonder what she feels, now,
listening to her recordings.

For they have already, within a few years,
begun to date . . .

Whatever they express
they express through the style of a decade
and a half—;
                    a style *she* helped create . . .

—She must know that now
she probably would *not* do a trill in
exactly that way,—
                          that the whole sound, atmosphere,
dramaturgy of her recordings

have just slightly become those of the past . . .

—Is it bitter? Does her soul
tell her

that she was an *idiot* ever to think
anything
              material wholly could satisfy? . . .

—Perhaps it says: *The only way*
to escape
the History of Styles

is not to have a body.

          •   •   •

When I open my eyes in the morning, my great
mystery
              stands before me . . .

—I *know* that I am intelligent; therefore

the inability not to fear food
day-and-night; this unending hunger
ten minutes after I have eaten . . .
                                        a childish
dread of eating; hunger which can have no cause,—

half my mind says that all this
is *demeaning* . . .

              Bread
for days on end
drives all real thought from my brain . . .

—Then I think, No. The ideal of being thin

conceals the ideal
not to have a body—;
                        which is NOT trivial . . .

This wish seems now as much a "given" of my existence

as the intolerable
fact that I am dark-complexioned; big-boned;
and once weighed
one hundred and sixty-five pounds . . .

—But then I think, *No.* That's too simple,—

without a body, who can
know himself at all?
                    Only by
acting; choosing; rejecting; have I
made myself—
                    discovered who and what *Ellen* can be . . .

—But then again I think, *NO.* This *I* is anterior

to name; gender; action;
fashion;
             MATTER ITSELF,—

. . . trying to stop my hunger with FOOD
is like trying to appease thirst
                              with ink.

       •   •   •

March 30. Result of the consultation: Both gentlemen
agree completely with my prognosis and doubt any thera-
peutic usefulness of commitment even more emphatically
than I. All three of us are agreed that it is not a case of
obsessional neurosis and not one of manic-depressive
psychosis, and that no definitely reliable therapy is
possible. We therefore resolved to give in to the patient's
demand for discharge.

       •   •   •

The train-ride yesterday
was far *worse* than I expected . . .

                                        In our compartment
were ordinary people: a student;
a woman; her child;—

they had ordinary bodies, pleasant faces;
                                        but I thought
I was surrounded by creatures

with the pathetic, desperate
desire to be *not* what they were:—

the student was short,
and carried his body as if forcing
it to be taller—;

the woman showed her gums when she smiled,
and often held her
hand up to hide them—;

the child
seemed to cry simply because it was
small; a dwarf, and helpless . . .

—I was hungry. I had insisted that my husband
not bring food . . .

After about thirty minutes, the woman
peeled an orange

to quiet the child. She put a section
into its mouth—;
                    immediately it spit it out.

The piece fell to the floor.

—She pushed it with her foot through the dirt
toward me
several inches.

My husband saw me staring
down at the piece . . .

—I didn't move; how I wanted
to reach out,
                and as if invisible

shove it in my mouth—;

my body
became rigid. As I stared at him,
I could see him staring

at me,—
      then he looked at the student—; at the woman—; then
back to me . . .

I didn't move.

—At last, he bent down, and
casually
            threw it out the window.

He looked away.

—I got up to leave the compartment, then
saw his face,—

his eyes
were red;
            and I saw

—I'm sure I saw—

disappointment.

•   •   •

On the third day of being home she is as if transformed.
At breakfast she eats butter and sugar, at noon she eats
so much that—for the first time in thirteen years!—she is
satisfied by her food and gets really full. At afternoon
coffee she eats chocolate creams and Easter eggs. She
takes a walk with her husband, reads poems, listens to
recordings, is in a positively festive mood, and all heavi-
ness seems to have fallen away from her. She writes
letters, the last one a letter to the fellow patient here to
whom she had become so attached. In the evening she
takes a lethal dose of poison, and on the following morn-
ing she is dead. "She looked as she had never looked in
life—calm and happy and peaceful."

•   •   •

Dearest.—I remember how
at eighteen,
              on hikes with friends, when
they rested, sitting down to joke or talk,

I circled
around them, afraid to hike ahead alone,

yet afraid to rest
when I was not yet truly thin.

You and, yes, my husband,—
you and he

have by degrees drawn me within the circle;
forced me to sit down at last on the ground.

I am grateful.

But something in me *refuses* it.

—How eager I have been ˌ
to compromise, to kill this *refuser,*—

but each compromise, each attempt
to poison an ideal
which often seemed to *me* sterile and unreal,

heightens my hunger.

I am crippled. I disappoint you.

Will you greet with anger, or
happiness,

the news which might well reach you
before this letter?

Your *Ellen.*

———————

Note: This poem is based on Ludwig Binswanger's "Der Fall Ellen West," translated by Werner M. Mendel and Joseph Lyons (Existence, *Basic Books*).

The Sacrifice

When Judas writes the history of SOLITUDE,—
. . .let him celebrate

Miss Mary Kenwood; who, without
help, placed her head in a plastic bag,

then locked herself
in a refrigerator.

●

—Six months earlier, after thirty years
teaching piano, she had watched

her mother slowly die of throat cancer.
Watched her *want* to die. . .

What once had given Mary life
in the end didn't want it.

Awake, her mother screamed for help to die.
—She felt

GUILTY. . . She knew that *all* men in these situations felt
innocent—; helpless—; yet guilty.

●

Christ knew the Secret. Betrayal
is necessary; as is woe for the betrayer.

The solution, Mary realized at last,
must be brought out of my own body.

Wiping away our sins, Christ stained us with his blood—;
to offer yourself, yet need *betrayal*, by *Judas*, before
                                        SHOULDERING

THE GUILT OF THE WORLD—;
. . .*Give me the courage not to need Judas.*

                    •

When Judas writes the history of solitude,
let him record

that to the friend who opened
the refrigerator, it seemed

death fought; before giving in.

Robert Bly

The Stump

The stump stands where it is easily overlooked until you come close. It is the size of a gray cannonbarrel, pointed up. Or an elephant's leg with the body shot off. Where bark is gone, something sleek and silvery shows, as when one glimpses an intestine. The stump feels rough to the fingers as a bandage, uneven as weeks of hospital introspection. Perhaps a giant's wooden leg, wounded. It ends in spires of rotted will, and broken-off vows, intentions we have not kept. Among the broken off vows, there is vegetation that grows in places inside us that we forget; these places are damp, surrounded by pine needles forgotten in the night.

Above the rooted stump that does not grow, the forest goes on growing, expanding, elaborating into the air. Vines climb trunks toward light. Wind goes over through high boughs. But there is something in life that doesn't know how to climb; it is sure everything around it that could help it go upward is dead, or unreliable. My great grandfather is with me as I stand by this unesteemed wood alone in the forest.

George Bogin

The Attaché Case

People look at me and say,
there's a man who knows
where he's going.
That's because of my
attaché case.
If I didn't carry it
who would notice me?
Entre nous,
it's filled with sand,
which is running out.

Philip Booth

Sorting It Out

At the table she used to sew at,
he uses his brass desk scissors
to cut up his shirt.
                  Not that the shirt
was that far gone: one ragged cuff,
one elbow through;
                  but here he is,
cutting away the collar
she long since turned.
                  What gets to him finally,
using his scissors like a bright claw,
is prying buttons off:
                  after they've leapt,
spinning the floor, he bends
to retrieve both sizes:
                  he intends to
save them in some small box; he knows
he has reason to save; if only he knew
where a small box
                  used to be kept.

Marianne Boruch

The Hammer Falls, Is Falling

All morning, the man roofs the house
he has dreamt the night before
walking with the wood in his hands
which is growing
as he holds it. The hammer falls, is
falling, one knee bent he
slams the nail
into its silence & out again into the great world
bird, rushing
out of sight, only
a black wing, the look of a wing
a glimpse of its darkness, nothing.
Stupid, he
bends his knee, stupid. Still the hammer
falls, is falling & the child
he dreamt, putting her to bed, closing the door
under the rude stars, is beginning
to wail, to call up
a word, the man hearing on the roof
the sound of the nail turned bird turned pupil of
darkness watching the air as though
it were breathing.

Joe Brainard

Nothing to Write Home About

Art Note

Painting a pear today, it occurs to me that what painting is really all about for me (at its best) is "discovery". The discovery of that third slight "bump" along-side the disappearing edge of the pear, which I had originally assumed was an almost straight line. However — the work itself eventually involved a sacrifice. And so what I ended up with was an almost straight line again. An almost straight line again, but with a very particular difference.

On Being A Gay Painter

Actually — I can't see that being a gay painter makes any difference what-so-ever, except that every now and then my work seems shockingly "sissy" to me.

Money

My idea about money is very similar to the gypsy idea about money: that a man's wealth is based not upon how much money he has, but upon how much money he has spent.

A Sign Of The Times

. . . are posters plastered up all over West Broadway advertising a new magazine called "No Magazine". Can hardly wait for the first issue! Seriously though — you know — aside from finding it all a bit silly, it's rather sweet too — don't you think? That we really care so much as to try so hard! And if the other side of the coin is "Why bother?"— that's exactly how I feel about the other side of this particular coin: why bother? If it's worth hearing, silence will say it better.

Breakfast Out

Out having breakfast this morning, over coffee, in somewhat of a slump (understatement of the year) I was thinking inside to myself: "Holy Shit, Joe — you'd better do *something* (anything!) to shape up your life a bit, or else!" (I.e., sink or swim.) And so I decided that — for starters — I'd try to be more out-going by trying to say something (anything!) to my waitress, other than my usual order and a "thank you" as it arrives. And so — as she was standing right in front of me, cleaning out a large white plastic container of some abstract sort — I opened up my mouth and out came "What's that?" But — (silence) — I guess she didn't hear me. Nevertheless, I gave myself a mini-pat on the back on my way home. A tiny "E" for a tiny effort. But with total faith that any step in the right direction is secretly a giant one.

Roaches

Let me tell you how I feel about roaches. I'm not crazy about roaches. But I don't hate roaches either. Just so long — that is — as they do what they're supposed to do. I mean like — it really doesn't bother me much to find them scurrying around when you turn the lights on. But when you turn the lights on and they *don't* scurry around, that really pisses me off!

New Plant

I like it. I don't *love* it. But I like it. It's . . . well, quite large. Or, rather, tall. About as tall as I am. Shooting straight up and out of a dark green plastic pot is a thin brown trunk that keeps going up and up until it finally "pineapples" out into many seemingly random directions. "Decidedly tropical" is the impression it gives. It reminds me of . . . well — truth be known — it looks like it belongs in a fancy restaurant. Or hotel lobby. At any rate — although I've never been a plant person — I do like it. Just the idea of having a plant around; I like that. And they're supposed to be good for the air. Though I've heard tell that *too* many plants can eat up *too* much oxygen in a room: hardly a pertinent problem as yet though. At any rate — it *is* nice to have a plant around. Though it doesn't exactly go along with the bachelor image I seem to have of myself: certainly a vision well worth dropping at this point anyway. How I happened by it was as a gift from a friend who decided to try the gypsy life for awhile: though more or less not by choice, to hear him tell it. Another nice thing about it is that, having chosen Sunday as its watering day, now I have something in particular to do every Sunday, which is a slight improvement over Sundays past. (It's never been my favorite day of the week.) Except for maybe Easter Sundays, when I was a kid. Though even that I'm not so sure of. New clothes were nice, but the hard boiled eggs *did* go on.

Rainy Sunday

This particular rainy Sunday (you know how Sundays are, so you know how *rainy* Sundays are) finds me torn. Torn between wishing I was spending the day in bed with someone cute and cuddly, and probably blond, or — then again — with some horny hot butch piece of meat. However, what I *am* in bed with is "Daniel Deronda" by George Eliot, which is awfully good really. And I didn't forget to water the plant today. And that tomorrow is Monday reminds me of how lucky I am that my time is my own (no regular job) and so tomorrow morning (thank God) won't find me wishing it was Friday again. And so now I can go back to "Daniel Deronda" with fewer complaints. How nice of *you* to be in my head to write to is!

Minor Freak-out

During Chapter 37 of "Daniel Deronda" my mind abstractly swerved onto (and into) the first time I distinctly remember hearing myself referred to as a man. Frederick did it. He said "I think you're a very handsome man." (Gasp!) Let me tell you — if it wasn't that we were in bed — I would have fallen on my face.

Thanksgiving

It seems to be that Thanksgiving is nearly upon us: another of my least favorite holidays. But — be that as it may be — I am wondering (and curious) as to what (if anything) Thanksgiving Day really "means" to me. Or, rather, what it makes me think of. And so now — (emptying out my head) — let's see what pops up. Well, first is turkey. Second is cranberry sauce. And third is "pilgrims".

Sexual Fantasy

Out through my window — across the way — and into another window — a bachelor man in white jockey shorts is standing (back to me) in the middle of the room with his legs slightly spread, in his bare feet: flat on the floor. The television set is on: a young blond Olympic swimmer in a black nylon bathing suit (so shiny from "wet all over") is being interviewed by an arm in a gray suit sleeve, microphone in hand. As a commercial comes on, he leaves the room. But soon (now) to return, with a beer in one hand (it must have been the kitchen) and his crotch in the other: "scratching" his balls with more than casual enthusiasm. Now . . . now he's slumping down into a low comfy chair, right in front of the set (T.V.) as the screen suddenly becomes a mirror, which suddenly becomes a movie. (Holy shit!) An X-rated movie — for sure — of this very humpy number (jocks down around ankles now) playing with his meat: big and hard and throbbingly hot. Now arching his body out straight as a board, his head falls back upside-down at me (big smile) on face as he shoots his load. As ivory streaks of cum fly through the air, I leak all over my feet.

Quaalude

Beauty and sadness and "landscape". The flow of time is so jerky, except in retrospect. Outside the window, I fall on my face in the snow: this is what I saw. And — suddenly — the whole sky goes blue: this is what I see. Beauty and sadness and "landscape": this is how I feel.

Insomnia

Now I lay me down to sleep. Or so I thought. Until my head began to open out onto everything and nothing in particular. Re-living random moments of the busy day, I feel cheated somehow. It all adds up to nothing, except this empty feeling I have inside, of just floating around through space. (What a waste!) What I want — what I need — is another body beside me now, to touch home base with. Someone to know for sure that I am "here" with. (What a boring drip you are, Joe!) These were my thoughts. Until I zeroed in on the inadequacies of this my particular pillow: too soft? Or too hard? And now neither my left or my right side seems quite "right" to lay upon. At least not for long. And arms — what to "do" with arms? Up and out of bed now — (fuck it!) — I like being naked, inside of a large dark space. (Like a cave man!) I like the cold hard floor on my bare feet. I like the way my balls swing freely as I walk around, back and forth. Why — out in the woods — I could squat for a shit as gracefully as any animal! Back in bed now, my eyes have found a place to rest. Upon the view outside my big front window: so silent and other-worldly out there. And the sky . . . it is so oddly colored: all greenish and lavender, with maybe a touch of orange. The color is "mud", but reassuringly "translucent". And now — having somehow found some comfort in all this — I am "myself" again enough to remember how mysteriously (no, how *un*-mysteriously) the "soon" of tomorrow will erase the "now" of tonight. Like a silent "Zap!" Surely one of life's kinder zaps — (those created by time) — they're being far too elusive to fall into. (?) All of which is going to seem pretty corny by morning, I suspect. But well worth buying tonight.

Oh My Gosh!
　　The gray hairs . . . they are streaming in at a most alarming rate. But by the light of my bathroom mirror, they gleam like silver. (Now how's *that* for trying to grow old gracefully?) Seriously though — I do have rather mixed feelings about being 36. (Mostly ranging from despair to horror.) "Help!": is *nothing* to be taken seriously anymore? Would you believe it? — I can't even confront myself in the mirror for a good balling-out session without a "foreign" grin slipping into my face. Which perhaps ought to be funny, except that it's too creepy. I mean like — who *is* that person? I don't know. (Three guesses who just had a birthday.) And so of course, I'm "milking" it. (But, really, I can't *afford* to let a little drama go by.) And so I *do* plead guilty, if only in fear of being accused of it. Not that I really care all that much any more. (Yes I do.) I'll tell you what is beginning to freak me out. It's that the older I get the more I miss . . . I think what

I miss most is who I thought was myself. That I will never be that clear again. That life will never be that simple again. I guess I fear the unknown, as much as I want it.

Right On!

Today I made a "Patience" sign to hang up on my wall. And, tomorrow, I plan to do a "Confidence" one. Because these are the two things I seem to want and need most in my life right now. And if I can't come by them honestly — fuck it — I'll learn how to fake it. As in *"Right On!"*

Sharon Bryan

Big Sheep Knocks You About

I've shorn over two hunn'ert in a day,
but big sheep knocks you about. I used
to go mad at it, twisting and turning
all night. Couldn't sleep after a rough
day with the sheep.

1

In town, in the foodshop, the men are making sandwiches,
cutting bread, cutting meat, cutting onions. The essence
of all these mixes with grease on their aprons, and
blood from cut thumbs. When they wipe their faces at night
it is to remember the day. They are good at what they do,
and beautiful to watch: silver, flesh, silver, flesh.

2

In the foodshop a boy with thick 15-year-old hands
is trying to help, but the bread breaks and mixes
with the bits of meat and sauce, though his hands
move after theirs the way a poem is said to be after
the Greek. They laugh, knowing they can teach him,
and his hands go on rising and falling like lungs.

The boy's hands on himself at night are surer, though
hurrying makes them clumsy, and shame that they should
be graceful at what they're doing. When his hands move
over a girl's body they are lost to him, so he dreams
of sea skates brushing coral. Of killing someone
without meaning to. His mother settling over his face
like a pillow. Home he makes himself come twice
before he can sleep.

3

And the boy's father dreams of England and Nettie
leaning fat against the wall with nothing on but
her stockings, saying Roll me 'round again dearie.
You know how I like it.

4

One stinks of blood and grease, flinty dead cells of hooves.
Two always face each other in profile, in the Greek
    curls of their horns and snouts and lips.
Three form a wedge that comes to a point just out of
    sight behind you.
Four run earnestly bunched in the same direction.
Five are not a team. They are dumb, they jostle and bump.
Six keep to themselves, just, in the crowd, avoiding
    each other with the grace of passivity.
Seven is used only by people.
Eight is not the seeds of dissent, these are sheep.
Nine is not the beginnings of mathematics.
Ten is a congregation with no preacher.
So is eleven.
Twelve has an unbreachable shape of its own,
    like a fertilized egg,
but at thirteen the edges begin to buckle and scallop,
at fourteen the sheep mill and mutter, and the dust
    rises to their ankles.
Beyond this the only shape comes from fences and short grass,
    humans circling, sheep circling.

5

In all the jokes it's the men who fuck sheep, drawn
to the puckery assholes, and it's perfectly natural
that Black Bart's girl is the wooliest. But when a
woman dreams of sheep, it's of the weight and thickness,
its penis stiff along the sheep's belly, steamy in
the cold, its horns spiralling invisibly in the dark.

The story of Leda was begun by a woman:. . . settling
over me, like the sky, and making my tongue swell
in my mouth . . . And ended by a man: . . . a bird, with air
in its bones. With eyes that see two things instead of one.

Michael Burkard

Star for a Glass

So many churches against the sky,
a small view beyond where a corner of the sea
converges with an even smaller landscape,
the spit less than motionless, as in a dream
where there's flame but not fire, where a child's cap
blows slowly across the street, where the land
ends where the street ends, and a man and a woman
turn their heads around.

Snowlight, a star for a glass.
I can still breathe. Although I have descended
too far into the April earth, I can still look up
and see the sky through the hole,
the one last snowfall in a light which must be
evening. To feed, to feed. To take your last name,
shout the name

— to walk out into nothing as the nighting is

Tom Clark

Lines Composed At Hope Ranch

Twist away the gates of steel
— Devo

O wide blossom-splashed private drives
Along which sullen mouthed little guys
In motorized surreys
Ride shotgun over spectacular philodendra!
O paradise of zombies!
O terminal antipathy to twist
And shout!
O hotel sized garages
Inside which smoothly tooled imported motors
Purr like big pussies under long polished hoods!
O fair haven of killjoys
United to keep surfers off
One of the great beach breaks
Of the West Coast!
O floral porticos, flowers
Of de Kooning, de Chirico
Chateaux! Estates where jokes
Aren't funny! What secret meaning awaits
Behind your stone & steel gates
Your walls of bougainvillea
Your date palm lined roads
Your quiet oak shaded lake
Like a European protectorate in Tanganyika?
Surely nothing disorderly, nothing disarrayed
Nothing at all except the great Pacific swell

Of money!

William Corbett

Edwin Dickinson's Perspective

Untimely alone.
Where are
the clothes I wore?
The South Wellfleet Inn
comes shuffling down
Is this the door
I came in before?
Sweet Christ, Edwin
you're dressed already
in your union blue.
I'm in here
with these industrial screws
down the woodland steps
a woman's torso
naked and bruised.
There is not a chair to sit in
but a chair to paint
and there is no air to breathe
in here: this is a poem to read.

My Uncle

My uncle had a birthmark
a liver colored flame on his face.
Who knows where that came from.

I remember one photograph
from 40's Hollywood, my uncle
Leo Carillo and a woman
who was not my aunt for long
and who was not
the English Duchess my uncle could have married
during the war.

The rest is one Sunday afternoon
visit to a second floor apartment.
It smelled of cooking.
I was five or six
when he last spoke to me.
He wouldn't know me now
if he fell over me.

Sam Cornish

Hometown

some-
times i am
a nigger
myself

i work
hard and i
                    say

what have

i   got

a child
learning
to play
piano

a wife
thats getting
older

i remember
my father

i remember
him crying

in a rocking
chair
                    facing

tea bags
and hot
water

Robert Creeley

Versions

after Hardy

Why would she come to him,
come to him,
in such disguise

to look again at him—
look again—
with vacant eyes—

and why the pain still,
the pain—
still useless to them—

as if to begin again—
again begin—
what had never been?

•

Why be
persistently
hurtful—
no truth
to tell
or wish to?
Why?

•

The weather's still grey
and the clouds gather
where they once walked
out together,

greeted the world with
a faint happiness,
watched it die
in the same place.

Age

He is thinking of everyone
he ever knew
in no order, lets
them come or go

as they will. He wonders
if he'll see them again,
if they'll remember him,
what they'll do.

There's no surprise now,
not the unexpected
as it had been. He's agreed
to being more settled.

Yet, like they say, as he
gets older, he knows
he won't expect it, not
the aches and pains.

He thinks he'll hate it
and when he does die
at last, he supposes
he still won't know it.

Robert Crum

A Child Explains Dying

First you close your eyes.
Then you hold your breath.

Then, when it gets too heavy to hold,
you let it go. And it drops to the floor
like a stone. But without a sound.

And then your mother comes to the door
and calls you, saying,
"Come out here this instant!
Your breakfast is cold."
And then your father comes to the door
and calls you, saying,
"No son of mine is going to lie
in bed all day. No son of mine
is going to be late for school."

And then they shake you,
and when you don't move
they see the mistake they made
and they cry and cry and cry.

And then they comb your hair
and brush your teeth
and dress you in a suit and tie
just like for Sunday School
And then they bury you in the dirt.

And your teacher gives your desk to someone else.
And your brothers wear your clothes
that you'll never need again
because you're a little lamb at the feet
of Jesus in Heaven—you're a little wooly thing
up in the clouds, going *baaa, baaa*.

Madeline DeFrees

New England Interlude

None of this seems real, seen from the east
and older. The red-eyed Guernsey bull,
his warning signal
stopped by the stooks of corn. This wilderness
is Thickly Settled
and the Berkshires' blue
surrounds my day.

           In Amherst, everything checked
in its fall: sacrificial stance of thistle,
flash of pumpkins in the field,
tomatoes stopped
on the withered vine. Here, tents
are made by caterpillars
or made of gauze and mean
shade-grown tobacco.

           Rococo time. The Rouault red
of fall: sculptured mastiff
chained to the barn door,
alert for the smallest opening. Mill Creek
low over the dam,
the sumac's plume still
red as the flag behind the final tee
at Cherry Hill.

           Into this flat sky,
western peaks lift their snowy desolations.
The chiselled legends call across my sleep. And will I

go back with the reddening salmon, escape
the long upstream of traffic,
my Nova rusted out, to a town in full view
of the sea?

What visionary company
follows the wale of water, crest and trough,
to hang on the seaward side
of Humbug Mountain?
A vertical drop, no breaker —
cut shelf for roadway, surf not dragging
shallow bottom, but slapping the face gently
where I ride the skiff of my body
into the seventh wave.

Stephen Dobyns

Spider Web

There are stories that unwind themselves as simply
as a ball of string. A man is on a plane between
New York and Denver. He sees his life
as moving along a straight line. Today here,
tomorrow there. The destination is not so
important as the progression itself. During lunch
he talks to the woman seated beside him.
She is from Baltimore, perhaps twenty years older.
It turns out she has had two children killed
by drunk drivers, two incidents fifteen
years apart. At first I wanted to die everyday,
she says, now I only want to die now and then.
Again and again, she tries to make her life
move forward in a straight line but it keeps
curving back to those two deaths, curves back
like a fishhook stuck through her gut. I guess
I'm lucky, she says, I have other children left.
They discuss books, horses; they talk about
different cities but each conversation keeps
returning to the fact of those deaths, as if
each conversation were a fall from a roof
and those two deaths were the ground itself—
a son and daughter, one five, one fourteen.
The plane lands, they separate. The man goes off
to his various meetings, but for several days
whenever he's at dinner or sitting around
in the evening, he says to whomever he is with,
You know, I met the saddest woman on the plane.
But he can't get it right, can't decide whether

she is sad or brave or what, can't describe
how the woman herself fought to keep the subject
straight, keep it from bending back to the fact
of the dead children, and then how she would
collapse and weep, then curse herself and
go at it again. After a week or so, the man
completes his work and returns home. Once more
he gathers up the threads of his life.
It's spring. The man works in his garden,
repairs all that is broken around his house.
He thinks of how a spider makes its web,
how the web is torn by people with brooms,
insects, rapacious birds; how the spider
rebuilds and rebuilds, until the wind
takes the web and flicks it
into heaven's blue and innocent immensity.

Susan Donnelly

That Time, That Country

In the country that was a time
I spoke in tongues,

a glossolalia of joy, like birdsong
in Beethoven's Sixth.

It was March in that country.
At the sign of the Lamb and Lion,

a chambermaid flings open a window.
That was the time

I shed the baggage
of extra flesh, to feel

frankness on my arms
that had been so wooden.

I forgave my city its grey
walls, shadows and gilt, bodies

rippling on the plateglass of stores.
For I saw him everywhere,

taking the form of strangers.
I came to believe

in corners, for what might lie
around them. What did I heed,

then, of the sad rush under my feet
as I watched carpets

shaken from high windows
like flags of state? And saw even doormen

look up at the cry
of wild geese beating their way

northward? A flower cart stood
at the curb, filled

with the crayon colors of childhood.
My countrymen opened to me

their individual faces.
As for the sky,

it had the look of the past,
but it shimmered with news.

Rita Dove

Taking In Wash

Papa called her Pearl when he came home
late, swaying as if the wind touched
only him. Towards winter his skin paled,
buckeye to ginger root, cold drawing
the yellow out. The Cherokee in him,
Mama said. Mama never changed:
when the dog crawled under the stove
and the back gate slammed, Mama hid
the laundry. Sheba barked as she barked
in snow or clover, a spoiled and ornery bitch.

She was Papa's girl,
black though she was. Once,
in winter, she walked through a dream
all the way down the stairs
to stop at the mirror, a beast
with stricken eyes
screaming the house awake. Tonight

every light hums, the kitchen is arctic
with sheets, Papa is making the hankies
sail. Her foot upon
a silk-stitched rose, she waits
until he turns, his smile sliding all over.
Mama a tight dark fist.
Touch that child
and I'll cut you down
just like the cedar of Lebanon.

Alan Dugan

Mock Translation from the Greek

Both Erato the Muse of Lyric Poetry and Mime
and Apollo the God of Poetry and Music
are said to be with us, in us, above us, and behind us,
and are often figured to be with a lyre, one
singing and playing with it, and the other
having it at her feet and waiting for action.
If you try to beat him in an arts-contest, he'll
skin you alive, the way he did Marsyas, that satyr
who was arrogant enough to challenge him once,
so you have to say, "God, let me have second prize
for my work, after you." Then he might nod,
if you're lucky, he might not even notice you,
if you're lucky, and if you do not listen to HER
when she comes up and talks in your ear,
whether kissingly or bitingly or just breathing something,
and if you don't listen and remember everything she says
or what you think she says, and get it all down,
anytime, anywhere, no matter what else is going on,
oh she will go away, either sadly, or amused, or furious,
or else with no human feelings at all, and leave you
with a mute in your mouth and a bug in your ear,
so you won't be able to hear her saying as she goes away,
                                        "You know
you stink. What you smell is your own upper lip.
It has to go. Take your last human breath of it, animal.
I'm telling your god Apollo to come down after you."

Russell Edson

The Melting

An old woman likes to melt her husband. She puts him in a melting device, and he pours out the other end in a hot bloody syrup, which she catches in a series of little husband molds.

What splatters on the floor the dog licks up.

When they have set she has seventeen little husbands. One she throws to the dog because the genitals didn't set right; too much like a vulva because of an air bubble.

Then there are sixteen naked little husbands standing in a row across the kitchen table.

She diddles them and they produce sixteen little erections.

She thinks she might melt her husband again. She likes melting him.

She might pour him into an even smaller series of husband molds . . .

On the Eating of Mice

A woman prepared a mouse for her husband's dinner, roasting it with a blueberry in its mouth.

At table he uses a dentist's pick and a surgeon's scalpel, bending over the tiny roastling with a jeweler's loupe . . .

Twenty years of this: curried mouse, garlic and butter mouse, mouse sautéed in its own fur, Salisbury mouse, mouse-in-the-trap, baked in the very trap that killed it, mouse tartare, mouse poached in menstrual blood at the full of the moon . . .

Twenty years of this, eating their way through the mice . . . And yet, not to forget, each night, one less vermin in the world . . .

David Ferry

At the Bus Stop; Eurydice

The old lady's face.
Who knows whose it was?
The bus slid by me.
Who in the world knows me?

She was amazed, amazed.
Can death really take me?
The bus went away.
It took the old lady away.

Ellery Street

How much too eloquent are the songs we sing:
nothing we tell will tell how beautiful is the body.

It does not belong
even to him or her who lives in it.

Beautiful the snail's body which it bears
laboriously in its way through the long garden.

The old lady who lives next door has terribly scarred legs;
she bears her body laboriously to the Laundromat.

There's a fat girl in the apartment across the street.
I can see her unhappiness in the flower she wears

in her hair; it blooms in her hair like a flower
in a garden, like a flower flowering in a dream

dreamed all night, a night-
blooming Cereus. A boy passes by, his bare

chest flashing like a shield in the summer air;
all conquering,

the king going to the drug store.
The snail crosses the garden in its dignified silence.

Rereading Old Writing

Looking back, the language scribbles.
What's hidden, having been said?
Almost everything? Thrilling to think
There was a secret there somewhere,
A bird singing in the heart's forest.

Two people sitting by a river;
Sunlight, shadow, some pretty trees;
Death dappling in the flowing water;
Beautiful to think about,
Romance inscrutable as music.

Out of the ground, in New Jersey, my mother's
Voice, toneless, wailing — beseeching?
Crying out nothing? A winter vapor,
Out of the urn, rising in the yellow
Air, an ashy smear on the page.

The quiet room floats on the waters,
Buoyed up gently on the daylight;
The branch I can see stirs a little;
Nothing to think about; writing
Is a way of being happy.

What's going to be in this place?
A person entering a room?
Saying something? Signaling?
Writing a formula on a blackboard.
Something not to be understood.

Caroline Finkelstein

My Father's Store

Lily's marking stock in the back
where Walter sweeps and bets
and makes boxes out of cardboard.
Rose at the cash dreams Cracow.
She's got numbers on her arm. Eleanor
threatens to call the union
if my father calls her fat once more.
     She's fat.

The code for thieves is nineteen;
when Pauline shouts *nineteen* aloud
everyone's eyes go *where* until they fall
on Pauline crooning *may I help you*
to someone in a big coat.
    A pig could fit in there.

Lily knows her husband is a bum.
She's marking stock and time, telling him
in her head he can go to hell with his blonde
for all she cares. She's hungry, too.

New goods are coming in!
Walter heaves the cartons down the stairs.
As my father dares him to be careful
Walter slaps stuff on the racks: scarves
and slacks, blouses from Hong Kong
     made wrong and all

to be discounted, men's furnishings
only in one color, thin silk dresses for a party,
for an evening, for a song —
            these stunning damaged things.

Hilene Flanzbaum

"Schools and Schoolmasters"

I used to watch your wrists in class;
the black hair curling on the backs of your hands,
your cuffs closing in small pearl buttons.
You chainsmoked, apologizing between cigarettes.
You waved the book at us, frustrated, yelling
the question—always the same question,
"Don't you see this? Don't you get this?"

Did you know all of the women in your classes
were in love with you? that we talked about it
all the time? I heard that a student
actually propositioned you and you said
you would have considered it, if you weren't
already married. For years I wondered if this
story could be true, and who the woman could be.

Before our conferences, I would stand outside
the office, sweating, planning what to say
to impress you—something so smart you would
want to sleep with me. But I always said
the wrong thing. I asked one day about
the wax whale on your desk—
"Is that Moby Dick?" (Four words to regret
forever) I had asked the man who had spent
his entire life studying Melville
if the white whale on his desk was Moby Dick.
But this is what you did to me—
made me talk too fast and without thinking.

Once, years after graduation, I saw you
in a restaurant, eating a sandwich,
talking to a man who looked comfortable.
I couldn't imagine what it would be like
to talk to you without suffering.
Even as I watched, my throat closed.
I walked over to your table—

You rose, shook my hand, and I blushed,
the deep red beginning at the base of my neck.
You did not ask me to sit down, so I stood
thigh against the table, saying some of the things
I had always imagined I would say if we met
like this—in a restaurant or on the street.
You wouldn't look at me, you hardly spoke.
As I walked away I remember thinking
I had done everything wrong.

Alice Fulton

From Our Mary To Me

I. As a child, Mary Callahan admired
    storybook orphans:
    Anne of Green Gables, Uncle Frank's Mary,
        transported
    from mingey asylums to wide-hearted strangers
    from skimpy wincey dresses to puff-sleeved splendors
    from boiled turnips to chocolate sweeties.
    And noticing that
    all orphans had blue-black hair and eyes and skin
    white as lace, she pictured them
    as consumptive Spaniards
    flaunting veils, roses, fans, Valentino's profile
    and somehow confused
    their juicy lives with Mary Daneher's: a rich girl
    whose carbonado hair,
    peaked complexion, yellow pink
    orchid and blue smocked dresses with hand-stitched
        collars
    lisle stockings and especially
    patent-banded tan suede high shoes
    and maid escort to St. Patrick's school
    seemed orphanesque and prevented
    our Mary from venturing near, much less daring
    a till-death-do-us-true-blue-kin-
    dred-spirit-ship, the way girls did in books.

    At night, our Mary read tales that made her blood
        jump,
    gazed through isenglass at the coalfire

and considered her own adventures: how she'd
crawled into the bull's pasture lost her drawers on the
    Green
Island Bridge kicked them in the river tapdancing
at the recital sat inside a freight car
talking to a tramp till it began to move
nearly taking her to Avonlea or Kalamazoo.

II. Mary Callahan, her daughter and her daughter's
    friend are talking about love and wealth and Mary
    Daneher. Our Mary says "I'd like to see her now
    to see if she has any smocking on her."
    The girls are memorizing every recipe in this month's
        McCalls
    because they haven't eaten in three days
    because they want to look thin in their minis and
        hipslingers.
    They are starving in hopes
    of having a yogic vision: a lost Beatle
    drives up in a psychedelic Rolls and proposes
    whimsical English sex. They are thumping
    their feet to imaginary drums and thinking
    if John Lennon loved them they'd be skinny
    though for that to happen they'd have to be.

    Hopeless! They are hopeless!
    I see their faces pinched with wishing
    and see them settling for the life they fight
    or a worse life they haven't bothered to consider.
    I don't know whether to love or fear them.
    From here I'd never find my way back
    to that fanatic state: upper New York
    Troy Michigan Deadend Avenue '67
    my mother saying "Cheer up, girls," swishing
    her housedress in a mad can-can, her legs
    brazening the air, her exit a "So there!"

flip of skirt, capework defiant as a toreador's,
leaving me weak with laughter —
the anemic daughter, stranger to her
than any waif or n'er do well
sat next to on a train, leaving me
neither her optimism nor charm,
only imagination, kicking
like a worm in a jumping bean.

Celia Gilbert

The Walk

"Don't go so fast," I called,
but my father always forgot.
Helpless, I reached to clutch
his coattails until his hand
surrounded mine and towed me on.

What knowledge of me did
his hand record?
What angers were given
to my childish keeping — to await
this instant, years later,

when I'm reproached: "Go slow."
Memories swell. He stops to rest.
A small victory implodes. So brief
the time before my child
will triumph over me
for hurts I caused, unknowing,
back on our deep-rutted road.

Lorrie Goldensohn

Letter For A Daughter

Put it this way, lovey, some people
stab themselves with their own strength:
stubbornly clinging, when all the best
of collective wisdom, not just your parents,
but your friends, too—calls up the feral
outline of a lover that love for yourself
should let you let go.

Thinking about it, I had it all
so clear in my mind, as placed above you
on this northern map, I wrote you good advice—
but the lines have wavered, and fallen short;
failing to touch that adolescent pride,
still hammer-firm in a southern city.
What lover could clear,

or should, the blackness from those eyes . . .
Wednesday, the pig came; we stacked it in boxes
by the door; the weather turned cold enough
to keep anything we wanted stiff. As in mute
promise, the pieces of the pig lay wrapped,
lay waiting for the festival of the returning child.
You didn't come.

By Thursday, hinting at spoils,
the massed disordered meat still lay
in its blood-stained papers, two greasy boxes
to be rendered into lard. At nightfall,
all of the burners covered with the big black

kettles and pots, we did it; swept up the floors
and put the cans away, warm oil

oozing in every crack of the littered stove,
as the large cans held their snowfall of fat
like deferred pleasure. His hair,
strained of color, holds you: the round, full
throbbing of that muscular neck, as it turns
in its senseless activity, the large hands
with the light blond fur, the blunt

nails knotting in the thickness of your hair,
quick and light in their ambiguous caresses,
hold you; tease and deploy us with the hopeful
possibility of our mistake—as nothing can be done—
our stomachs full of the veteran pig, the six months
since we saw you. The river in back of the house
clarifies. Slowly and carefully, the snow

thins from the winter-scabbed path. All things
drive to their opposite number. My life
hunkering down in your youth, as absently,
you blur towards a stale body—fresh error—snow
gives way to the black slick mud, and the sky
lightens. Sunday, that bald signal, augmenting,

reaches round for its repeating self again.

Jorie Graham

I Was Taught Three

names for the tree facing my window
almost within reach, elastic

with squirrels, memory banks, homes.
Castagno took itself to heart, its pods

like urchins clung to where they landed
claiming every bit of shadow

at the hem. *Chassagne,* on windier days,
nervous in taffeta gowns,

whispering, on the verge of being
anarchic, though well bred.

And then *chestnut,* whipped pale and clean
by all the inner reservoirs

called upon to do their even share of work.
It was not the kind of tree

got at by default—imagine that—not one
in which the only remaining leaf

was loyal. No, this
was all first person, and I

was the stem, holding within myself the whole
bouquet of three

at once given and received: smallest roadmaps
of coincidence. What is the idea

that governs blossoming? The human tree
clothed with its nouns, or this one

just outside my window promising more firmly
than can be named

that it will reach my sill eventually, the leaves
silent as suppressed desires, and I

a name among them.

Kimono

The woman on the other side
  of the evergreens
a small boy is hidden in,
  I'm wearing
valleys, clear skies,
  thawing banks

narcissus and hollow reeds
  break through.
It means the world to him, this flat
  archaic fabric
no weather worries.
  Each time I bend,

brushing my hair, a bird
  has just dipped
through its sky out of
  sight. He thinks
I don't see him, my little man
  no more than seven

catching his lost stitch of breath. . .
  What he sees,
in my garden, is the style
  of the world
as she brushes her hair
  eternally beyond

the casual crumbling forms
   of branches. I bend
and the reeds are suddenly
   ravines. . .How soothing
it is, this enchanted gap, this tiny
   eternal

delay which is our knowing,
   our flesh.
How late it is, I think,
   bending,
in this world we have mis-
   taken. Late

for the green scrim to be
   such an open
door. And yet, even now, a small
   spirit accurate
as new ice is climbing
   into the gentle limbs

of an evergreen, the scent rubbing off
   on his elbows
and knees, his eyes a sacred store
   of dares,
to watch, as on the other side,
   just past

the abstract branches, something
   most whole
loosens her stays,
   pretending she's alone. . . .

Allen Grossman

The Department

Siste, viator

Bereaved of mind by a weird truck,
Our fraternal philosopher
To whom a Spring snow was mortal
Winter— a wild driver in the best
Of cases, on the margins of
Communicability— exchanged a bad
Appointment in New Hampshire
For a grave in the Jewish Cemetery
In Waltham, Massachusetts. Across
The street from the University
And nine feet from Philip Rahv
He keeps his hours, perished
With little fame.

His name was Boime.

"A very heavy business, Grossman"
He would have said,
If he had heard his own death going
The way it did.

Immortality
Was our Summer debate. But in the snow's
Confusion blurring definitions
Darkened into mortal blows. Consider
The wit
Of circumstance which made that mind— alive

Unwriting, and naive—
Record its own demise on paper
As a flat brain wave.

                    Who speaks for
Boime for whom
The University found just this much
Room?

        His subject was the violence
Of mind, and the duplicity of his kind.
There was a wound, he thought, deeper
Than doubt where love

                  could enter, or
Look out—
Weary of the faithless civil compromise.
But that was not the wound of which he died.
He was a lousy driver who got caught.

An idle woman looked out on his burial
From her window
In the salmon colored house—

                   a disharmonious fact
Between the cemetery and South Street—
Sitting on a bed.
Nothing can be said, except

                  the passionate
Theorist is dead. In death he was
Unclear—

His aged father, like a gouged up root;
The bitter wife; the child of five
Who wondered how his dad would ever
Get out of that box alive;
The bearded bandits who cranked him down
Know as much as I do,

                or anyone.
He left his work unfinished. Whether
It was good or bad nobody knows—
It was not done.

            Somebody is digging
On your grave, dear Boime,
Who in that snowfall, when you died,
Was farther South than you,
Better employed.

            Your name is
Pencilled in now on a tinny bracket
By a casual hand. A baby
Has been buried at your side.

                Since you
Died
It is the second Spring,
And nobody has set up your stone.

                  God
God what a big
Thought, Boime, you carried into middle age—
Fat gladiator, treacherously caught
By a suffocating thin snow, chained
To a careening metal cage.

I am digging on your grave, like a starved
Dog burying a fact—

     If I say, "Boime, you
Were abstract,"

    then with a great sweet
Smile, even from among the dead,
Who don't know anything, he will reply,
Leaning a little toward the Summer

       under
His unbalanced cloudly load,
And with his lovely gesture of the hand,
"Grossman, you do not understand
The place of theory.

    Get off the road."

The Thrush Relinquished

One night there was no moon, and never had been.
In the space where the moon was

                                the weather
Stopped, everything happened for
The first time.

                   I cannot imagine space
As it then was, the cradle unrocking
In the tideless air.
The man stopped, the shadow vanished,
There was nothing to read.

In their yellow groves the midnight villas
Went dark, as if the timid sleepers put
Out the fear lights, the dark being no more
"The dark." Patience in me ceased to betray
Itself by tears.

The poet is dead, and from his stare released
The stars weary of dance divest themselves
Of countenance.

                No poetry tonight. Death tonight.
The thrush relinquished, my hand is in the open.
I can see every way.

David Gullette

Angling

In advance, much deconstruction and rebuilding.
You guess what each part must do at a crucial moment
then memorize the whole. If every click is not dreamlike
you take it down again. Much bathing
of stars and rings and springs in clear solvents.
Letters with numbered codes and curious names go out
at night to distant factories: Send One of Each.
The table is littered with bits of possibility:
they await your refitting — nothing too tight, too slack.
You ask, Can I throw out my mind, and retrieve it?

At last the day comes, you rise before dawn
to disinter the long sleepers or dice up the dead.
As for the place, you know in general but not exactly
which rock, ledge, spit or jetty will say ME
like a face from a former life. When you're certain
what needs to be strong is strong, what sharp, sharp,
and your murderous steel concealed in temptation,
you take your pose, pause, swivel and send
the transparent filament arc-ing out into
the swirling enigma mapped only by the drowned.

You scrunch down into your vigil — long or short,
who knows? You cradle your rod, it comforts you,
even the pillow of stone is soft enough, you sleep
and see the dark kingdom of the underworld,
the vague shapes drifting aloof — those you have
insufficiently loved turning away in bitterness, in sorrow:
and you wake to the last of the line racing out,
something unforeseeably large is pulling away
and you brace yourself for the loss, too late
too late to slow it: snap.

Donald Hall

The Henyard Round

1.

From the dark yard by the sheep barn the cock crowed
to the sun's pale
spectral foreblossoming eastward in June,
crowed,
        and crowed
later each day through fall and winter, this grand
conquistador of January drifts,
this almost-useless vain strutter
with wild monomaniac eye, burnished swollen chest,
yellow feet serpent-scaled, and bloodred comb,
who mounted with a mighty flutter
his busy hens: Generalissimo Rooster
of nobody's army.
               When he was old we cut his head off
on the sheepyard choppingblock, watching his drummajor
prance, his last resplendent march . . .
As I saw him diminish, as we plucked each feathery badge,
cut off his legs, gutted him,
and boiled him three hours for our fricasse Sunday
dinner, I understood
How the Mighty are Fallen, and my great-uncle Luther,
who remembered the Civil War,
risen from rest after his morning's sermon, asked
God's blessing on our food.

2.

At the depot in April, parcel post went cheep-cheep
in big rectangular cardboard boxes, each
trembling with fifty chicks. When we opened
the carton in the cool toolshed
fifty downed fluffers cheep-cheeping
rolled and teetered.

                  All summer it was my chore
to feed and water them.
Twice a day I emptied a fouled pan
and freshened it from the trough; twice a day
I trudged up hill to the grainshed, filled
sapbuckets at wooden tubs and poured
pale grain into v-shaped feeders, watching the greedy
fluster and shove.
            One summer
I nursed a blind chick six weeks — pale yellow,
frail, tentative, meek,
who never ate except when I gapped space for her.
I watched her grow little by little,
but every day outpaced
by the healthy beaks that seized feed
to grow monstrous — and one morning
discovered her dead: meatless, incorrigible. . .

3.

At summer's end the small roosters
departed by truck, squawking with reason. Pullets
moved to the henhouse and extruded each day
new eggs, harvested morning and night. Hens roosted
in darkness locked from skunk and fox,
and let out at dawn footed the brittle yard,
tilting on stiff legs to peck the corncob
clean, to gobble turnip peels, carrot tops, even
the shells of yesterday's eggs. Hens labored
to fill eggboxes the eggman shipped
to Boston, and to provide our breakfast, gathered
at the square table.
                    When the eggmaking frenzy
ceased, with each in her own time set
for weeks as if setting itself made eggs,
each used-up diligent hen
danced on the packed soil of the henyard her final
headless jig, and boiled
in her pale shape featherless as an egg,
                                        consumed —
like the blind chick; like Nannie
who died one winter at eighty-seven, childish,
deaf, unable to feed herself, demented . . .

Anne Halley

Rumors Of The Turning Wheel

I lived among a people
who said, pig, for luck. They might have said stork or
    flounder
for these beings were familiar to them,
as were rat and donkey.
But they said, pig. No doubt from ingrained habit.

Real pig, fella. Some pig you had, my friend.
What pig. Good pig! Hey, have a piggy day.

In the city they sent post cards
printed with pink snouty
fat pigs in frock coats, usually eating sirloin,
and they pasted
elegant gold pig-shapes on party hats and crackers
while some embroidered piglets dancing in a ring on
    tea-cloths
or pinned ceramic pigs with wings on their firm, tailor-
    made lapels.

Things were different in the country. Money too tight
for fancy toys and gew-gaws. The Pastor stern
in the distribution of lamb. They made their good sausage
and all had pig, quietly. Sparrow, mouse, and child
with some further diminutives continued
a respectable tradition of endearments
although every real man knew
that at the proper moment one forgets himself, unbends,
    shouts: Pigtail!

Marzipan pigs by the Kilo
with clever curly tails are still exchanged at New Year's.

The usage, inherited and hallowed,
survived famine, pest, vast shifts in population.
I've heard few inquiries about it. Among us here
in the new, open land the custom decayed, remembered
     perhaps
as rumor for children: the ghost of the clay
piggy you feed for a year until it bloats, fills up with coin
and then you get to smash it. Fringe groups and
     malcontents abound
and some return
to the koshering that is a silence.
Lately I've had reports
of gigantic chocolate pigs in our most exclusive
suburban shops. They challenge the carver's knife
on paper frills, discretely air-conditioned. Somehow I find
them difficult to swallow. A cheap nostalgia. Bad pig.

Mark Halliday

Blue Spruce

I've got a feeling
that moves me deep inside
oh yeah
I've got a feeling
I think I'll put it into verse
oh yeah
in fact this feeling of mine is almost an idea,
or a pair of ideas with a feeling attached,
or rather the two ideas swim in the feeling
like eccentric bathers in a tub of blue honey.

I could put my feeling into prose, I suppose —
at least, I think I could tie down
my pair of ideas fairly firmly
in a well-built paragraph or two,
lashing them with qualifiers;
and the feeling surely would hover loyally
around the edges of the paragraphs,
wouldn't it? Like a butterfly nuzzling
two perfectly even rows of random flowers —
it would be there somewhere, the feeling,
and meanwhile the ideas would be so definite,
so definitely *there*,
I would have gotten them down,
down, down
like a strangled wrestler.
Professors of Applied Math would respect me at last!

Except —
now that we get right down to it —
I'm not all *that* sure exactly
what my ideas are. I know what they're *next* to,
I think, but when I stare right at them —
like distant stars, you know . . .
If you want the truth, it's as if
the two ideas have to be dissolved
in the feeling, and if you vaporize that
you're left with a clammy precipitate, a small soggy lump
unworthy of meditation . . . Still,
I guess I could get close to the real stuff
in maybe a dozen paragraphs, by saying
all this, and doubling back to re-tie the knots —
I admit it, in conscientious prose
I could pin down up to 98% of my real meaning,
buttoning its collar, tucking in its tails, weaving
the arduous network of responsible reference —

but who wants to?
Where is the fun in all that expository disquisition?
Poetry is so much more enjoyable
in about seven or seventeen ways!

Notably, when I write some half-decent verse
everyone allows me to feel I'm special;
amazingly, this is still the case even when
there are nearly a thousand other poets
just in my own greater metropolitan area —
we're still special, because
everybody writes prose,
including your dental hygienist, probably,
and the hyper-bourgeois president of your Alumni
        Association.
Secondly, — and here's the real charmer
among the attractions of verse:

it's so much *easier* to write than prose!
Poets don't admit this, of course,
and why should they?
If they're not going to get paid
they should at least be allowed to
milk the public for a little respect;
and in this country people respect *work*.
That's right, I said work,
and no funny business. So a versifier,
in order to win any lasting respect
(beyond the glow of a few chuckles)
has got to seem to labor.
Yet the secret fact of the matter is,
as indicated above, that verse is no sweat,
relatively speaking; because

you don't have to plug all the holes;
in fact, you're supposed to
                              punch out
new ones;
you can leave loose ends dangling
all
over the
          bed,
                    the
kitchen table,
               your lover's
                              body,
your
      parents' lives,
and people accept them as part of your game.
In verse there is no final judge,
and they know it, and you know they know it,
and as long as you tie up every fifth string,
roughly, your readers and listeners will imagine
that some of the other four strings

are *probably* tied up, and who knows which?
Oh, it's a fine life, this making verses;
PROSE IS SERFDOM;
in poetry the freedom is a blast.

             ("Blast" . . . Do I mean that metaphorically?
             Do I intend some ironic overtone of explosion?
             Or is "blast" here simply a colloquial term
             which I resort to for a touch of comic relief?)

Just leave them baffled
and they'll treat you right!
It's so easy when you get the knack,
I could die laughing about it sometimes —

the way you can take them out on a ledge
at the end of your poem
and give them a little shove —
nobody has a right to ask you why —
and off they go

sailing through the charged air
like a betrayed mountaineer
plummeting from the track
of some communal trek
falling free of all social ropes
tasting the murderously rushing bracing beautiful air
and landing
            far below
apparently unhurt
though stunned
in the limbs of a blue spruce
                   and staring
into the calm wild eyes of a meadowlark
who offers no lucid advice
but releases
an aerial stream of clear and liquid notes.

Functional Poem

Is there any reason why a poem shouldn't
at least occasionally
come through for us in a concrete way and
get something done?

Because I need to get something across
to a particular individual
with whom I have no normal contact,
I mean I never see this guy, and yet
I've got something to say to him —
and me being a poet I naturally
have to use
the means at my disposal.

The individual to whom I refer
is a young man with blond hair,
I admit from a certain point of view
many people would consider him handsome although
he's what I call rather heavy-set i.e.
chubby. Well-dressed, the guy has money, I'm sure
he wears those yellow-white cotton pants
made for people like golfers and princes
who can take everything slow and cool —
not that he does. Because

the one time I saw this guy
on a hot inter-suburban street some years ago
he was driving his white Camaro
with his radio on terrifically loud with
some old Beach Boys song which I normally like
but it seemed a sacrilege for this rich guy to have
that old gentle light-hearted music in his Camaro —

the song was a hit when this character was about
five years old, for god's sake! —
but anyway he cuts right in front of me,
I'm driving my father's old VW,
he almost clips my fender, gives me this look,
like "You're over the hill, man, get off the road" —
I'm under 35 and this guy is telling me
I'm over the hill! So naturally
I give him a blast on the horn.
So then the bastard slows way way down.
So I pass him, except all of a sudden
he speeds up to keep even with me,
I'm stuck out in the left lane
and here comes a frigging truck or something!
So I hit the brakes and duck in behind him
in his beautiful creamy white Camaro
with the Beach Boys and a little cooler of
Miller High Life in the back seat, I'm sure.
Almost immediately he does the slow-down thing again —

and this time he lets me pass him.
But then about thirty seconds later
vrrrroooooommm! — he's passing me
but there's traffic coming toward us,
God, my heart seized up like a broken clutch —
but
he made it, the bastard,
I admit he had great acceleration,
and nerve, too, the guy had nerve —
he pulled away into the distance,
going even faster to show me that
the near miss never scared him for a second.

Okay. Now, I've thought it over,
and I realize that what's wrong with this individual
is not that he's rich, or that he's young,

or that he's a little on the heavy side.
That stuff is his business, and the same goes
for the loud radio as far as I'm concerned and
the fast driving too, even, in most situations.
But what's wrong with the guy is
that he made me run the risk of
severe damage to life and limb or
possibly a fatality, i.e. I could have been killed.
And that is just not acceptable.
I'm saying, this person cannot be permitted
to do such a thing.

Now, I know all your theories, by the way,
about "Poetry makes nothing happen"
and art is not a tool or weapon et cetera.
But on the other hand it *is* a way of giving messages,
and if I'm being a little more honest about this
than most poets, then so be it;
and I'm just giving that blond individual
this message:

Don't go around interfering with somebody else's
right to live, you stupid jerk.
Why don't you consider some other life-style
less dangerous to others and yourself as well?
Why don't you read some poetry once in a while?
If this poem can do a job on you,
maybe others can, too. Why don't you
take some of your gas money and
subscribe to a few poetry magazines?
Think about it.

Readers, if you see the above individual,
or somebody like him, could you
please just pass along this message.

Paul Hannigan

Fiesta

Just as I was about to call your name
The phone rang
And since I was alone I knew it must
At last be you

I thought: the times are trying to change us
Into trees in the valley of the shadow of joy
But all the blessings which flow from memories of you
Seem to represent the x in Mexico
Mention of which nowhere appears in the Holy Bible
Another inexplicable oversight on the part of God's
Otherwise tireless writers
With wingspans of up to seventeen feet
And faces which caused the blood to run
So cold as to produce rime on the armor
Of certain holy knights

But parts of any magic occasionally fail
It was not you
It was a disappointing surprise
A wrong number from Mexico City named Perez
Intent on reaching his sister Julia
Something about a disturbing telegram from her
Beginning Aiyee Querido Hermano
As Mexican telegrams are said to do

Like a tree sinking deeper
Every day into your absence
Which fills all but an insignificant corner
Of the known world I hung up
After Perez and heard
A cry in the street
In the manner of ballads
A child's blanket fell past my window
No one in it I knew
Caught my eye
The whole thing taking less than
A minute in my calm life

Study Aids

I
In learning a foreign language
Leave a red mark by each word
You look up in the dictionary

When you look up a word
And find a red mark by it
Cut off one joint of your finger
With the dullest possible knife

II
In mathematics try to remember
That the answer is always
A multiple of 1

And the method
Some version of slyness
Common knowledge to
Stone age louts

III
In philosophy when your teacher
Cannot explain to your satisfaction
Feign a heart attack

As he kneels
Over your body
Spit in his face

IV
In theology
Constant smiling
Frequent head noddings
Everything is true

Everything is gorgeously true
True ten thousand times
Sit in your seat or on the floor
Or the ceiling or the teacher's eyelash

V
In learning your own language
There will be words you can never learn
Cut them from the pages
With a razor

Swallow the paper
Choke on it
Envy the termite
And the silverfish

William Harmon

Mother-land'scape (Letters)

Dear Mother dear,

Now this here's an Edda,
which in Icelandic means "greatgrandmother."

Snorri's *Skáldskaparmál:* well, Aristotle's *Poetix* it ain't,
not by a googolplex of parsecs, no ma'am;
nor is the *Gylfaginning* any *Iliad* or Exodus.

But our northern temper (born of winter nights
on the iced bridge, bred and borne
on the vast namelessness of ocean stretching and yawning
far from the mistfinks and bastard toadflax of the world
      of Rome)
goes for the hard words and bony notions —
                              Ginnungagap!
                              Jörmungandr! . . .

Here now's how Hárr told Gangleri about Heimdallr:

The White God!
Nine sisters gave Him birth!
Hallinskidi, Gullintanni, many names!

Solid gold teeth!
His horse is called Gold Top!
His dwelling goes by the name Hininsbjörg, next door to
      Bifrost!

The Gods' own tyler, he sits by the bridge at Heaven's end
to keep watch for Hill-Giants!
Needs less sleep than a veritable bird!
Sees, night and day alike, things 100 leagues away!

Can hear grass grow on the earth, wool on sheep!
His trumpet Gjallar-Horn's alarm-blast calls all galaxies!
Heimdallr's sword is called Head!

   * * *

No score and seven years back
I called myself the gross national prod.
I take it all back. This is my palinode.

He Himself in *Heimdalar-galdr* has it:
I am of nine mothers the offspring,
Of sisters nine am I the son! . . .

And consider, Mother, consider the Silent God.
Consider Vídarr.
He has a thick shoe!

And O my dear Mother, consider Hárr's words on Doom:

One day, after the World's Worst Winter,
And after Axe Age and Sword Age, after the spell
Of shields split in brother-murder, Wind Age,
Slaughter of daughter by father, the smoking stars,
Day of the falling-down Earth, horizon crazy awry,

Voluminous wolves swallowing sun and moon,
Then will come the bad ship *Naglfar,* the dreadnought
Made out of dead men's fingernails!

(Take note, undertakers: for a corpse to go to its grave
Without a proper manicure

Adds just that much more raw *matériel* —
From keel's "swine" to hatches' "dogs" — for *Naglfar*;
And nobody, man or God, is in any hurry to have
The Dragon-figured battlewagon go sliding down the ways.)

Well, it will come when it will come, old *Naglfar,*
Manned by punishments,
The heavy nail-helm minded by the giant Hrymr,
The great pale stern lettered
                    N A G L F A R

And at the grinning water-line
The warning
                    TWIN SCREWS   KEEP CLEAR

Psychosomatic piety from infancy is not bad,
but David and Augustine are my models.
Bring on the Bathshebas and Carthages,
the peaches and the pearly pears!

                    *   *   *

These sentences relinquish elegance as they gain weight,
but gravity itself can shed an elegance;
                              Dear Mother —
when my father did away with himself in February 1947
he left us nothing but ourselves — a widow of forty
with an only child of eight — in a parody of marriage,

a Theban Eden according to some paradigms, an ideal
        matrix:
I had you to myself without knowing that that
was what I was supposed to want to have.
It was not what I wanted. I wanted a father.
You wanted a husband. (Not that he — another
William Harmon in the world — was necessarily
the man we needed, but he served well enough awhile.)

The other day a friend said, "You go everywhere twice.
I've even been to Bora Bora twice."

I write more poems about women than anybody should.
A mother, a wife, a daughter, a secretary, women around
    all day—
I say
how sorry I am things are the way they are.

O a tremendous travesty, a burlesque of love
according to Jung-Alfred Prüfstein,
a man talking to himself, the auto-prose houdini'd
into a "love"-"song"—

                    Where did I get the idea, years ago,
to write a Dialogue on Dutch Light?
Austerity more exciting than something tropical,
Rectilinear Calvinist prose, Mondrian's room, or
        Wittgenstein's,
bare northern habits of work,
Auden faithfully paying his bills on the day they came in,
a clear eye on the bank balance and classical prosody,
each day squared
by square-faced clock and calendar—
dear Mother—
                utter order,
and silence, and whiteness
of the uncomplicated steady-state rose
of heaven or of hell. . . .

                        white housepaint
                        grit-grey scouring powder
                        dark-gold tobacco
                        chocolate

It seems so stupid
to be hungry for hunger,
such a deciduous phenomenon,

the passing of time in time,
the tick *edax rerum,*

and the indeterminate preview in the bone
of death's death's . . . death,
the last number odd —

odds and no ends!

(next day:)
                          Our subsidy has come through.
Now we are subsidized,
now we can do as we please,
now we are like farmers, shipping lines,
railroads, magazines.

At 5 o'clock this morning
I dreamed I saw a king cobra
on top of the kitchen cabinet
and woke up with one loud abrupt vowel
and stayed awake
not thinking of the menace
of your having lost twenty pounds in two months
without trying to
(even though you should have done so long ago,
down now from 165 to 145)—

the involuntary loss, however happy,
is no good for a woman within ten days
of her sixty-seventh birthday.
When I said "Take care of yourself" I wasn't kidding.

. . . Egad, a year has passed, and this has not been mailed!

*   *   *

THE DRAGON-FIRE-PRIEST

Straight (dear mother)
The chain of jewels reaches from the sun
To the priest's heart
And when at midnight lamentation or noon
        thanksgiving
He opens his mouth to sing
The many-colored light there born becomes our holy
        melody
And the Dragonwords so become our holy harmony
That the perfect spun chain of jewels, returning,
Reaches from here as far again as the orbit of the
        woven sun himself,
To and fro,
And the execution of that pattern (dear
Mother) constitutes the figure of the dance.

The nuns dance, the mothers dance,
And the old men dance in the dark light falling
Between the wine and the moon;
The belles dance between the old men and the
        moon
Until the moon, dead overhead at midnight himself,
        changes the dance,
The dance changes, the wives and husbands change
        in time.

The priest is a king, the song is the perfect key,
An ancient secret that accompanied the Ancestors
When they travelled across the scales from the
        greater stars —

In Dragoncraft came they with their emblematic
    Dragonaxes!—
To establish here a faithful colony
Where the long roots end and the earthly waters
    start.

Now the hammers (dear mother) have danced on
    their anvils.
There is nothing between our people and the stars.

The bonedance necklaces are flung into the fire
(There is nothing between our people and the stars),
The belles dance naked now Dragonshadows fall
    from the midnight moon.

Today I held your Dragongrandson.
I touched his leg and said the immemorial word
    shin.
The model of the bone is millions of years old.
The mother of the word is millions of years old:
    shin!

Our Dragondaughter writes on the altar too:
A poem begins the world and a poem will end it.

Michael S. Harper

Chief

*For those who are neither hero of myth nor
witness to history: remember all life is holy.*

In the year of the blizzard
in the month of February
I have traipsed up the middle
of Lexington Avenue, a spectacular
middle passage in the snow
to my own poetry reading:
James Wright, Philip Levine,
each having written about a horse,
neither a hero of myth
nor witness to history alone,
nor a palamino looking for a drink.

I could be water, or fire,
and on earth, which is covered with snow,
there is a bar where the air is filled with snow:
the air from my lungs billows in the fog
of my own friendly breath
as I walk down into the subway
into a labyrinthine holiday of dreams
and a *book of nightmares*
which I carry under my arm
signed by the author, Galway Kinnell,
after his introduction of Etheridge Knight
and me, a high contrast in poetics,
and the politics of light, and the smell
of the one horse I did ride
in Central Park after a girl.

Chief is my hour and my dark horse:
he does not belong to me, or to Crazy Horse,
who was caught by a bullet or a noose
because he was too quick for the camera,
the transcendant Lakota, Enchanted One,
whose name leaps from enchantment
to a horse eating in the snow.
One searches for the meaning of the railroad
and the buffalo, and the hidden names of the horse,

In a blizzard, under martial law, and alone
in Providence, holed up in one office on George St.,
no easy street, and no snowplow, and no horse
to tread the rudders of a delivery truck
on the milk route, or the ice-wagon of my childhood,
or the stubble at the end of my mistress's hand
in the Central Park waterway of the horse.
A mixture of oats and honey, raw carrot
and a moving picture camera of children
riding in the snow. I have loved this image
of a horse running over the plains of Scott
Momaday's "Plainview: 1 & 2"
and the detention of a horse in a mindless barn
of a friend, and once for the ridden part
of a season of horse in a park
where no child was the air of a poetry
reading, or the middle passage of survival,
which put name on the horse,
a camera on the man who rides the image,
and a hero as a witness to the woman
who rides him.

Jim Harrison

from Returning to Earth

> "What forgotten reverie, what initiation
> it may be, separated wisdom from the
> monastery and, creating Merlin, joined
> it to passion?"
>
> Yeats, *A Vision*

She
pulls the sheet of this dance
across me
then runs, staking
the corners far out at sea.

* * *

O I'm lucky
got a car that starts almost everyday
tho I want a new yellow Chevy pick-up
got two letters today
and I'd rather have three
have a lovely wife
but want all the pretty ones
got three white hawks in the barn
but want a Himalayan eagle
have a planet in the basement
but would prefer the moon in the granary
have the northern lights
but want the Southern Cross.

* * *

My left eye is nearly blind.
No words have ever been read with it.
Not that the eye is virgin — thirty years ago
it was punctured by glass. In everything
it sees a pastel mist. The poster of Chief Joseph
could be King Kong, Hong Kong, a naked lady riding
a donkey into Salinas, Kansas. A war atrocity.
This eye is the perfect art critic. This eye
is a perfect lover saying bodies don't matter,
it is the voice. This eye can make a lightbulb
into the moon when it chooses. Once a year I open
it to the full moon out in the pasture and yell
white light white light.

* * *

Disease!
My prostate beating & pulsing
down there like a frightened turkey's heart.

* * *

Mandrill, "Mandrillus sphinx,"
crest, mane, beard, yellow, purple, green,
a large fierce, gregarious baboon
has small wit but ties himself to a typewriter
with wolfish and bloody appetite.
He is just one, thousands will follow,
something true to be found among the countless
millions of typed pages. There's a picture
of him in Tibet though no mandrills have been known
to live there. He wants to be with his picture
though there's no way to get there. So he types.
So he dreams *lupanar lupanar lupanar*
brothels with steam and white dust, music
that describes undiscovered constellations
so precisely the astronomers of the next century

will know where to look. Peaches dripping light.
Lupanar. The female arriving in dreams is unique,
not another like her on earth; she's created for a moment.
It only happens one time. One time O one time.
He types. She's his only real food.
O *lupanar* of dreams.

* * *

What sways us is not each other
but our dumb insistent pulse beating
I was I am I will I was
sometimes operatic, then in church
or bar-room tenor, drunkenly, in prayer,
slowly in the confusion of dreams
but the same tripartite, the three
of being here trailing off into itself,
no finale any more than a beginning
until all of us lay buried
in the stupefying ache of caskets.

* * *

Living all my life with a totally normal sized dick
(cf. the authorities, Van Velde, Masters & Johnson)
neither hedgehog or horse, neither emu or elephant
(saw one in Kenya, the girls said o my goodness)
neither wharf rat, arrogant buck dinosaur,
prepotent swan, ground squirrel, Lauxmont Admiral
famous holstein bull who sired 200,000 artificially.
I am saved from trying to punish anyone,
from confusing it with a gun, harpoon, cannon, sword,
cudgel, Louisville Slugger. It just sits there
in the dark, shy and friendly
like the new kid at school.

* * *

He sneaks up on the temple slowly at noon.
He's so slow it seems like it's taking years.
Now his hands are on a pillar, the fingers
encircling it, with only the tips inside the gate.

* * *

Abel always votes.
Cain usually thinks better of it
knowing not very deep in his heart
that no one deserves to be encouraged.
Abel has a good job & is a responsible screw,
but many intelligent women seem drawn
to Crazy Horse, a descendant of Cain,
even if he only gets off his buffalo pony
once a year to throw stones at the moon.
Of course these women marry Abel but at bars and parties
they are the first to turn to the opening door
to see who is coming in.

* * *

O my darling sister
O she crossed over
she's crossed over
is planted now near her father
six feet under earth's skin —
their still point on this whirling earth
now and I think forever.

* * *

Beatrice Hawley

The Marsh

You make yourself new again.
Along your sides,
only a thin line marks the scar
where you lay open one whole summer.

Steam rises from your body
in this heat.
You move slowly
you sit up to your chin in yourself.

One morning you are a blue floor.
You are rising, you are learning
to walk again, your feet do not stumble
over the wide roots.

The birds come back,
they tear at you, opening their beaks
in hunger, you feed them.
They will stay.

Again the salt burns in your blood,
but your mud is soft
and you are walking towards the sea.

Seamus Heaney

A Kite for Michael and Christopher

All through that Sunday afternoon
a kite flew above the Sunday,
a tightened drumhead, an armful of blown chaff.

I'd seen it gray and slippy in the making,
I'd tapped it when it dried out white and stiff,
I'd tied the bows of newspaper
along its six-foot tail.

But now it was far up like a small black lark
and now it dragged as if the bellied string
were a wet rope hauled upon
to lift a shoal.

My friend says that the human soul
is about the weight of a snipe
yet the soul at anchor there,
the string that sags and ascends,
weighs like a furrow assumed into the heavens.

Before the kite plunges down into the wood
and this line goes useless
take it in your two hands, boys, and feel
the strumming, rooted, long-tailed pull of grief.
You were born fit for it.
Stand in here in front of me
and take the strain.

Near Anahorish

I.

I stood between them,
the one with his tawny intelligence
and fencer's containment,
his speech like a bowstring,

and another, unshorn and bewildered
in the tubs of his wellingtons,
smiling at me for help,
faced with this stranger I'd brought him.

II.

Then the cunning voice of poetry
came out of the wood across the road
saying, "Be adept and be dialect,
tell of this wind coming past the zinc hut,
call me sweetbriar after the rain
or snowberries cooled in the fog.
But love the cut of this travelled one
and call me also the cornfield of Boaz.
Go beyond what's reliable
in all that keeps pleading and pleading,
these eyes and puddles and stones;
and recollect how bold you were
when I first visited you
with betrayals you cannot renege on."

from Sweeney Astray

Sweeney Astray is a version of the Middle Irish tale, *Buile Shuibhne,* in which Sweeney, king of a small kingdom in north-east Ulster, is cursed by a saint and transformed into a bird at the Battle of Moira. The bulk of the story is concerned with his subsequent life of frightened wandering and resourceful complaint.

22.   Sweeney kept going until he reached the church at Swim-two-Birds on the Shannon, which is now called Cloonburren; he arrived there on a Friday, to be exact. The clerics of the church were singing nones, women were beating flax and one was giving birth to a child.
         — It is most unseemly, said Sweeney, for the women to violate the Lord's fast day. That woman beating the flax reminds me of our beating at Moira. Then he heard the vesper-bell ringing and said,
         — The echo of the cuckoo's voice on the banks of the Bann would be sweeter than the whinge of this bell here to-night.
Then he uttered the poem:

23.   I perched for rest, and imagined
cuckoos calling across water,
the Bann cuckoo, calling sweeter
than church bells that whinge and grind.

Friday is the wrong day, woman,
for you to give birth to a son,
the day when Mad Sweeney fasts
for love of God, in penitence.

Do not just discount me. Listen.
At Moira my tribe was beaten,
beetled, heckled, hammered down,
like flax being scutched by these women.

From the cliff at Lough Diolar
to Derry Colmcille
I saw the great swans, heard their calls
sweetly rebuking wars and battles.

From lonely clifftops, the stag
bells and makes the whole glen shake
and re-echo. I am ravished.
Unearthly sweetness shakes my breast.

O Christ, the loving and the sinless,
hear my prayer, attend, O Christ,
and let nothing separate us.
Blend me forever in your sweetness.

Anthony Hecht

A Lot of Night Music

Even a Pyrrhonist
Who knows only that he can never know
    (But adores a paradox)
Would admit it's getting dark. Pale as a wrist-
    Watch numeral glow,
Fireflies build a sky among the phlox,

    Imparting their faint light
Conservatively only to themselves.
    Earthmurk and flowerscent
Sweeten the homes of ants. Comes on the night
    When the mind rockets and delves
In blind hyperboles of its own bent.

    Above, the moon at large,
Muse-goddess, slightly polluted by the runs
    Of American astronauts,
(Poor, poxxed Diana, laid open to the charge
    Of social Acteons)
Mildly solicits our petty cash and thoughts.

    At once with their votive mites,
Out of the woods and woodwork poets come,
    Hauling their truths and booty,
Each one a Phosphor, writing by his own lights,
    And with a diesel hum
Of mosquitoes or priests, proffer their wordy duty.

They speak in tongues, no doubt;
High glossolalia, runic gibberish.
    Some are like desert saints,
Wheat-germ ascetics, draped in pelt and clout.
    Some come in schools, like fish.
These make their litany of dark complaints;

    Those laugh and rejoice
At liberation from the bonds of gender,
    Race, morals and mind,
As well as meter, rhyme and the human voice.
    Still others strive to render
The crossword world in perfectly declined

    Pronouns, starting with ME.
Yet there are honest voices to be heard:
    The crickets keep their vigil
Among the grass; in some invisible tree
    Anonymously a bird
Whistles a fioritura, a light, vestigial

    Reminder of a time,
An Aesopic age, when all the beasts were moral
    And taught their ways to men;
Some herbal dream, some chlorophyll sublime
    In which Apollo's laurel
Blooms in a world made innocent again.

Richard Howard

Howard's Way

A Letter to 102 Boulevard Haussmann

Mon cher maître, could even you have mastered
such dissemblance?
                    Given your gift for luring
the accidental and the inevitable
to lie down together, what would you have done
with these disparities—could you have parsed them
into a semblance of sense?
                          Mind, that phoenix,
kindles its own fire: identity at stake,
it does not depend on the world for fuel—
must I? Dear Marcel, did you?
                            Suppose I rehearse
how it went with me last night, how far it went
beyond my means: I write what I recover from
what I have chosen to forget. I put it
to you—perhaps you can put it right for me.
No one knows the ropes better, what lines to draw,
what chords to strike, what strings to pull—and knowing,
for better or worse, would tell.
                                Now just suppose
you had accompanied me, had paid a call
in answer to a call, a summons from hell—
as any place is hell, at the other end
of a telephone wire, that is not heaven.
Suppose you approached, with *your* urbanity,
my city's most publicized apartment-house
looming grim at the Park's edge, grimy and grand—

sufficiently grand to be used for shooting
horror-movies.
                    (I know, you cannot have heard
of horror-movies. Or can you? *Fantomas*
was shown in Paris, you saw *Judex, La Proie* . . .
Seeing is believing—we are what we see,
and if what we see and believe is silly,
only what we could see, could believe is not.)

Horror-movies then, and there—could you believe?
in the redoubt Dakota, so huge our word
apartment takes on a meaning all its own,
the converse of togetherness (now that word
you never heard of, thank God. We mean well, but
the ease with which we say what we mean—horrors!
sounds like the most affable of lies).
                    To the dark
Dakota then you came, suppose, and instead
of visiting its most Proustian denizen,
the leading lady famous not for her roles
but for her first appearance in a Southern
hamlet, also the birthplace that very year
(and the hideout since) of the one novelist
we've had who takes after your own hidden heart—
though knowing another man's secret is not
the same as having to live with your own . . .

Suppose, then, rather than visiting "the girl
next door" to our great fabulist, you had found
yourself and me outside another door, one
to an attic room, really a *chambre de bonne*
(more likely, in the Dakota, *de mauvaise*)
bestowed by that lady on her kissing kin,
the man who called us, whom we are calling on!

He famous as well: the poet-pornographer
freshly returned—restored—a pilgrim from Nepal
and beautiful, still beautiful, or worse still
you could see that he had been beautiful once.
He admits us, the old beau, with a hard look,
as though wondering how much we cost. (*He* cost
a lot, and can afford to be entertaining
only to strangers: entertainment at best
is merely lust compassionately disguised
as the will to please.
                           Master, you *are* helping!)

Pattering across the parquet, his blind pug
attacks. "Down, Principe, down! Oh dear, do mind
that pile of poo." We bestride the pool of pee
by inches, whereupon we are well inside
a room filled (or emptied) by a flickering
blue light. There are others here, oblivious
of Principe and us: all their faces turned
one way, washed by a reflected radiance—
mysterious little male presences, looking
just like pressed flowers.
                           We sit down too, we watch.
On the screen, persons inconceivably wound
around each other commit by noose and knout
actions of ecstasy and passions of pain
on a hairless Oriental boy, a child!
though is that a child's body? relentlessly
acquiescent to the penetrations of
a grey-haired man . . .
                           All at once another man,
corpulent, with the face of a polite snake
(the man who uses all the instruments) comes:
there is a sudden struggle, until both men . . .
The child's hand flutters, though they hold him down, **and**
two fingers thrust across the screen in protest

or appeal: black talons, inches long.
                                No one
speaks. Not a word. Only the reel chatters on—
the bodies exchange a last seizure, comic,
anonymous. To forego identity
as these do, first give up the fear of falling—
most of us cannot, for who would need to rise
if we were not afraid of falling?
                          By this
light or lack of it, the little audience
has the look of men watching and unaware
we are watching them watch: a look as though
they were not in their own bodies, but in ours . . .

Something breaks, the screen goes blank, and here we are
sitting with a dozen men in a room so
nondescript no reasonable person could
possibly make love here, or commit suicide:
keeping up appearances is not difficult
once you have seen through them—you told us, master,
merely hold them from behind, the way you hold
a shield, and appearances protect you quite well.

Introductions follow: the guest of honor,
a tall, grey-haired man of ash and addictions
whose first forbidden book everyone devoured;
the later licit ones are, of course, unread:
the one way we can survive is to become
imitations of ourselves—for otherwise
experience touches us and we must change.

Beside him, his sarcous secretary whose
pale eyes are so wide-set that like a serpent
he can look straight ahead only by turning
his face from side to side.
                          And across the room
a third person is identified, though hardly:

a living idol, fourteen perhaps, and so
symmetrical he need not have a self . . .
                                             "This
is Inda, I brought him back from Katmandu."
I hold out my hand as he does, the idol does,
and then I feel the nails. So he is the child,
those are the men—he suffered, they were there then,
here now: grey hair, snake eyes . . .
                                   Horror-films, indeed—
we take off our sex and have . . . clothes! I cannot
bear this. Master, is art the image of life?
Is life?
        "Act your age," you urge me and, outraged,
I answer: "What is acting? I should act yours,
you mean—one more obscene performance . . ."
                                               You
take your part by holding your peace. You are not
there, you are silent—have you left me?
                                   Rudely,
I admit, I stumble, almost running, out,
unready for that recognition scene . . .
                                   Down,
away! where winter opens the clouds above
the Park and beyond the trees. There are the stars,
unsteady constellations—blue movies all
right, or all wrong: a world whose beauty is just
a jangle to our ears, a blur in our eyes,
an entanglement about our feet . . .
                                   I move
by darkness as *they* moved by light: Howard's way.
Crossing the city to send you this, I am
awed as the meanings converge, syllables
I cannot dispel, alien oracles
I cannot receive: Dakota. Katmandu.
                                   Richard

Fanny Howe

Onlie X

The constant X
equals all variables:
even strangers soon to be wonders
just amount to X.

Cistercians, all 'sister', in any case
sexless, insist
the last & best
is left for X.

So Wilde's little swallow
made children cry, don't fly!

But action is prayer
for the poor and/or
ill; just makes equal
stone and jewel.

And X—
to everything else than X—
is just as much more.

Poem For Potential

All-sufficing person
come alive again!

Light's at attention—
polite at the end of
the sea. High gold
& celibate, a bold
celestial glare — Here.

Sharks in the pines,
the park shines.
This isn't the only time.

Once before you stood on
a hill of sand — wind
in your child-like hair —
blowing, blown!

Susan Howe

Sonnets

come in light variable and with calm
good weather most of the time
on the floor of my house silence
a round a pond the bush a hush
hilldog Bark and horseprint calm
cold like a crescent moon
a hunter rode alone through snow
possessed of supernatural powers
composed of rags and tatters
Forest closed and gently
rolled away the door to years
a tell tale compass   brass knuckles

and Death   death of everyone born
comes in light variable   comes in calm

                    *

a man holds an object
the position of his hand
has the effect of a gesture
toward his wife who holds a flower
                    wrote letters read etc.
wrote letters read etc.
all that golden afternoon
across her face the hills grew tight
he had wanted to marry his mother
conversation soon died altogether
holding a wide awake or quite full face

with forks and hope   she had gone elsewhere
exposure left only the faint image
                on the page
in which we appear as if splashed

                        *

I came to the garden long ago
under beam and fleck   at cock-crow
under comets and new stars
I was looking for something in sand

I learned all the laws of inertia
then gave my notes to a friend
in a minute it would slam down rain
his forest turned with his face

we talked of the white wedge of wonder
of space and time and the echo of brass
my signature did the talking for me

my father's wings were folded under the table
that was the really appalling thing
there in the sunlight when his forest
                        turned with his face

1974

Richard Hugo

1805 Gratiot

1.

If I had to guess, I'd say
some other house, and some street
less arterial. Nothing's at my back
and east seems arbitrary as coin.
Dawn might come anywhere in this flat land
bewildering as elms and horses,
Twenty-nine years after his class
and thirteen after his death
I'm here to pick up the prize named for him.
I try to guess the greenhouse, the path
he ran across the field, how Gratiot looked when dirt.
Leaves from two maples in front snap
under my step and the house stands locked
in some white dignity that doesn't fit.

I went to Forest Lawn. The dead were quiet as stone.
I saw a dog that didn't mean other.
I saw a chain of flower shops with his name.

> Gilliflower, who?
> Gilliflower, whee.
> That's three thousand bucks
> they're giving me.

Too many ponds are filled in.
Wind, what happened to the slime, the eye
of an alien friend nailing a small boy hard to the day?
What happened to the blinding dazzle of glass,

the hurt rat hoping for help, the steam
that starts all things, day, eye, drift of cloud
and river?
It is October.
I am walking on his leaves.

2.

The right thing does not always happen
to the happy man who must be unhappy
to find the next poem.
Rivers, even the slow Saginaw, move on.
Spirit of weather
can't we name a bridge right once?
Does the dog wait at the field's edge for nothing
but his howl returned by a wall of trees?
I fashioned a life from failure.

What's in the sand?
Only the wind.
What's in the wind?
The beggar's hand.

Where was the path?
I asked the mole. He said, turn blue.
Luck, luck, luck sings the willow.
I hear a ghost grunt.
He can't break out.

3.

Birds came stampeding. Light
from the sea came hard in my eyes
and I was running alone
where only words could validate

thunder's exterior fear and the interior sea floor,
blue pulse on rock, dark cirrus, dark stratus,
one horse and acres of grass, mountains
where elk maintain their own meadows,
the sky where seabirds cut outlines
of women who fill out warm in cold light,
wave hello and are gone.

Fish and rivers to name, and a sad man
went to one river on Sundays.
The air was rich gray. A green rain
fell all week.

Here I must not whisper of the tough death
of leaves appropriated by a mid-west autumn for mulch.
When he died I found he was more to me
than I'd thought,
the boy ghost climbing to that porch.

> Where's the ear?
> The ear's in the fear.
> No one came to the door
> when I knocked hard.

4.

When light comes hard what it is to suffer
a sky that murmurs like earlier sky.
Another day. What does it matter?

I can't expect the answer from my doctor.
There I am, twelve, alone on the rim of the bay
when light comes hard. What it is to suffer

the tide because the high must be to be lower.
I passed my physical o.k.
Another day. What does it matter

I'm over fifty. I'm happier than ever.
Whatever the tide, the moon is always high.
When light comes hard, what it is to suffer

sight of the end, to know that over and over
no word's right to welcome warmly
another day. What does it matter

when light comes hard what it is to suffer
another day? What does it matter?
Reports marked negative pour in. Every day
one past can still give way to another.

5.

To have come this east,
the walk, the full wind
bearing down on the gravelbed,
the eye spiraling slowly,
a slow leaf-twirling, momentous;
To be by the house
climbing brightly out of the lawn,
huge as a man in his first awkwardness;
To see natural line become harder in mid-day sealight,
and fog shifting, wafting out of the blue sea lanes;
To look into the after-this, the laser left on the sea's margin
where the sun has collapsed back of a stiff horizon;
To follow the stones laid out by a gifted ear,
love's tongue, when the poet raves and the brief day moves
        utterly seaward;
To know what words gang and ring, often without our doing,
as a mature rain fills to the edge of the bay's basin,
stops and rages at the rim, then turns back to lower,
due again to freshen the roots of the thirsty lover.

6.

Twenty-nine years.
Thirteen
Off the right wing
Lake Michigan's resolute blue
goes out of sight north like ocean.
I remember what he said: nothing
matters, nothing, not prizes, publication
or applause, nothing but the writing.

When I try my next poem
he'll be right again.
A nation he loved passes below
slower than it passes from a train.
Backstage last night, Ciardi was touching.
I remember the standing ovation.
For me, old teacher.
For me.

David Ignatow

The Fly

I killed a fly
and laid my weapon next to it
as one lays the weapon of a dead hero
beside his body — the fly
that tries to mount the window
to its top; that was born out of a swamp
to die in a bold effort beyond itself,
and I am he that brought it to an end.
Tired of the day and with night coming on
I lay my body down beside the fly.

Phyllis Janowitz

Let's All Get Up

When your house is smashed by an avalanche,
and in the family room, where only minutes ago
you were watching General Hospital, you lie

moaning, crisscrossed with ribbons of wood
and wool, until hours later an Airedale
pulls you out by one ankle, do you get up

in the snow and tap-dance? You know,
in a plaster cast from chin to toe, it's
not fun to sing Hallelujah. Unable to move

the tin man and I would make a fine team
if we could reach over, weave our twin
hands together. In the meantime, my feet

take root in the back yard dirt, the body
withers, my arms shed leaf by dry leaf.
Trapped in the interior a finch

beats bruised wings, as if it remembered
swooping down and ascending on a soft
current of air. Then the wind, the rain,

the mailman arriving from Barcelona to say
the children are fine. The travelers.
Flowering transplants dazed by the rough

tongue of the sun and the smell of tar
and the sting of brine. Oh casaba melon,
rind of lemon, flittering jacana!

It is not possible to forget.
From the bare branches of myself —
our house, our home — rising out of

chair legs and dinnerware, the crumbling
rubble of kitchen and attic, the ranting
rabble and riff-raff of departmental

officialdom; declawed, hairless,
missing teeth, I smile, knowing that
somewhere in Spain, somewhere in Portugal

Hackensack or Poughkeepsie, they will see me
waving my fingerless arms
and they'll wave back.

Although I am Taking Courses
in the Language

Although I am taking courses in the language
of children, penguin socialization
and creative writing, now, in my dotage —

dotage, what a striking word — I find
myself betrayed — betrayed — by what?
Betrayed! That's what it means to be human.

First acceptance, then rage, then reiteration.
Once dinner was always exactly at seven.
We said a prayer. Naturally, I imagined

my grandchildren would have red hair and make
kipful good as my own. I didn't think they'd
arrive right off the green farms of Alpha Centuri

out of touch, wearing headphones and refusing
to move without tape decks and wide receivers.
Exhausting, their tolerance for a drifting world.

How can I get through to them? Listen, listen
I want to say (as if it would make a difference)
without order there can be no love, not even

tenderness, the only possible purpose
under a dying sun — the only one.
My hearing grows worse with the years;

what passes from human to human is inaudible,
yet how clearly I hear what they hear. Fragile
and pale, Humpty-Dumpty bounces on his wall

in the sky, high on the timeliest twaddling tunes
and worlds may break to bits, worlds may be reglued.
I nod and sigh. What else can I do?

It is not to me, alone, the little
angels cry, *Come to dust Come to dust*
The sun has ten billion years to go.

Visiting Rites

We drive up the winding road
lined by graying sycamores,
a blessing in the summer heat.

At a small table, between
the stones, a man and two women
nibble crustless sandwiches,

pour from a silver pot of tea.
They have their arrangements:
dour frigidity of gladioli,

faded dresses, a musty gentility.
We have brought a few daisies,
short-lived and casual.

It's a matter of style, Mother says.
Days of water, days of sun put
circles in the trees. A green-

glass summer lies in pieces. It is
afternoon. We watch the women
pack their picnic away. Counting

Live, die, live, die
Mother assigns white petals
to a mound of earth. Something

hidden but familiar will repeat
the same design — it is not
a question of illness or cure.

If I could refuse such whispers,
such sighs, I'd fold the long
shawls of mourning, give up

descendants, prayer — all
kinds of fixed hooks — be single
as an angel, dancing and blind.

Jane Kenyon

Frost Flowers

Sap withdraws from the upper reaches
of maples; the squirrel digs deeper
and deeper in the moss
to bury the acorns that fall
all around, distracting him.

I'm out here in the dusk,
tired from teaching and a little drunk,
where the wild asters, last blossoms
of the season, straggle uphill.
Frost flowers, I've heard them called.
The white ones have yellow centers
at first: later they darken
to a rosy copper. They're mostly done.
Then the blue ones come on. It's blue
all around me now, though the color
has left with the sun.

My sarcasm wounded a student today.
Afterward I heard him running down the stairs.

There is no one at home but me —
and I'm not at home; I'm up here on the hill,
looking at the dark windows below.
Let them be dark. Some large bird
calls down-mountain — a cry
astonishingly loud, distressing. . . .

You were cruel to him: it is a bitter thing.
The air is damp and cold,
and by now you are a little hungry....
The squirrel is high in the oak,
gone to his nest, and night has silenced
the last loud rupture of the calm.

Camp Evergreen

The boats like huge bright birds
sail back when someone calls them;
the small campers struggle out
and climb the hill to lunch.
I see the last dawdler
vanish in a ridge of trees.

The whole valley sighs
in the haze and heat of noon. Far out
a fish astounds the air, falls back
into its element. From the marshy cove
a bullfrog offers thoughts
on the proper limits of ambition.

An hour passes. Piano music
floats toward me over the water, falters,
begins again, falters. . . .
Only work will make it right.

Some small thing I can't quite see
clatters down through the leafy dome.
Now it is high summer: the solstice:
longed-for, possessed, luxurious, and sad.

What Came to Me

I took the last
dusty piece of china
out of the barrel.
It was your gravy boat,
with a hard, brown
drop of gravy still
on the porcelain lip.
I grieved for you then
as I never had before.

Bill Knott

Poem

Our eyes unlash slowly one
by one at last bald lids rise

What for

Mimicry
re
the poet's eye
looking inwards sees
without the lashes' soft-pleaded intercedence
too pupilly cool cruel
as muttered justice

I call my goodbyes home in the
dusk

Breeze Nomadly Coupling)
Summer Sounds
(Precision Insects Chomping

As much as someone could plow in one day
They called an acre
As much as a person could die in one instant
A lifetime — scoot over a little,

The greatbig instuments, click up to measure
Stress in constellations and in navels everywhere —
      tremor-
Lorn sharp antennaed as lovers' hissing lips
That can gauge the remotest substitution of self
      instant,ly —
                        till it's as if

Nothing is left — for them to record but other
Devices, nothing, an orchard of juicy sideswipes, this air:
      finest
Steeply-rooted sensor, which tinguely

Transcends its meters, like handtinted
Applause, inching, miling, monthing, nighting
Ultraserene, — across our lost, shiver-boundried bodies . . .

The Stillborn (Domesticity #3)

Eyelashes did their job:
they lengthened the afternoon,
like a dress hem.

Then that night the hem began to rise, in stages
revealing
scenes from my shameful life.

Those calves
up which the hem reproachfully rasped,
catching,
lingering over the ugh pictures
did belong to a woman

or were they mine—
I hid my eyes.
I wouldn't attend to
the walls either

endless walls, slowly
basted
with suicide.

The eyelashes did their job.
But I, who could neither sew
nor cook groped and groped those long legs
stubborn, afraid to look.

Yusef Komunyakaa

More Girl Than Boy

You'll always be my friend.
Is that clear, Robert Lee?
We go beyond the weighing
of each other's words,
hand on a shoulder,
go beyond the color of hair.
Playing Down the Man on the Field
we embraced each other before
I discovered girls.
You taught me a heavy love
for jazz, how words can hurt
more than a quick jab.
Something there's no word for
saved us from the streets.

Night's pale horse
rode you past commonsense,
but you made it home from Chicago.
So many dreams dead.
All the man-sweet gigs
meant absolutely nothing.
Welcome back to earth, Robert.
You always could make that piano
talk like somebody's mama.

Maxine Kumin

How to Survive Nuclear War

after reading Ibuse's *Black Rain*

Brought low in Kyoto
too sick with chills and fever
to take the bullet train to Hiroshima
I am jolted out of this geography
pursued by Nazis, kidnapped, stranded
when the dam bursts, my life
always in someone else's hands.
Room service brings me tea and aspirin.

This week the Holy Radish
Festival. Pure white daikons
one foot long grace all the city's shrines.
Earlier a celebration for the souls
of insects farmers may have trampled on
while bringing in the harvest.
Now shall I repent?
I kill to keep whatever
pleases me. Last summer
to save the raspberries
I immolated hundreds of coppery
Japanese beetles.

In some respects
Ibuse tells me
radiation sickness is less
terrible than cancer. The hair
comes out in patches. Teeth
break off like matchsticks

at the gumline but the loss
is painless. Burned skin itches,
peels away in strips.
Everywhere the black rain fell
it stained the flesh like a tattoo.
Weeks later when survivors must expel
day by day in little pisses
the membrane lining their bladders
pain becomes an extreme grammar.

I understand we did this.
I understand
we may do this again
before it is done to us.
In case it is thought of
to do to us.

Just now the homage that
I could not pay the irradiated dead
gives rise to a dream.
In it, a festival to mourn
the ritual maiming of the ginkgo,
pollarding that lops all natural growth
from the tumorous stump
years of pruning creates. I note
that these faggots are burned.
I observe that the smoke
is swallowed with great ceremony.
Thereupon I see
that every severed shoot comes back,
takes on a human form,
fan-shaped, ancient, all-knowing,
tattered like us.

This means
we are all to be rescued.

Though we eat animals
and wear their skins,
though we crack mountains
and insert rockets in them

this signifies
we will burn and go up.
We will be burned and come back.

I wake naked, parched,
my skin striped by sunlight.
Under my window
a line of old ginkgos hunkers down.
The new sprouts that break from
their armless shoulders are
the enemies of despair.

Brad Leithauser

The Life-Giving

With nothing but God's word
to go on, I built
a boat too big to move,
that never would float
unless the sea came
climbing the hills to take it.
And even before the clouds
had fully swollen, I loaded
my live, paired cargo and waited
for the expanding seas
to find me. For nearly
six weeks the rain held up,
and—man and animal—we
huddled in the hold, itching
with straw until the tap
of rain on wood was no longer
something we noticed. And after
the rain, left in the lurch
and drop of water, we floated
for a full year across the sea-flats,
looking for anything more solid
than our own rocking ship.
I tallied the dull, choppy days
into my log, using words which,
eventually, began to sound like names
of animals—the peeves and pledges,
the tiny squabbles and runaway fears.
Nevertheless, I believed
in us, in our floating barn
and the land which finally steadied our vision.

But when, at last, light
spilled through an opening,
and God revealed his capsized arc
in a vast band of colors bent
like a bubble over the sea,
I found something to stun me:
my shipmates, my seaworthies,
the animals themselves, newly
alive in the light—the shelled
and feathered, the racers, the logy,
the insurmountable masses,
the slithering legless, the egg-layers,
the mud-colored clay-crawlers,
and a whole team of craftsmen . . .
spinners and weavers and tiny carpenters!
To a brain that finally caught fire
they seemed creatures made in my own images,
the images of a mind shaped
(as rock itself is finally shaped)
by the incessant wear of water;
like creatures created from dolor and downpour
to rise and answer the falling sky.

Denise Levertov

Gathered at the River

For Beatrice Hawley and John Jagel

As if the trees were not indifferent . . .

A breeze flutters the candles but the trees give off
a sense of listening, of hush.

The dust of August on their leaves.
But it grows dark. Their dark green
is something known about, not seen.

But summer twilight takes away
only color, not form. The tree-forms,
massive trunks and the great domed heads,
leaning in towards us, are visible,

a half-circle of attention.

They listen because the war
we speak of, the human war with ourselves,

the war against earth,
against nature,
is a war against them.

The words are spoken
of those who survived a while,
living shadowgraphs, eyes fixed forever
on witnessed horror,

who survived to give
testimony, that no-one
may plead ignorance.
Contra naturam. The trees,
the trees are not indifferent.

We intone together, *Never again,*

we stand in a circle,
singing, speaking, making vows,

remembering the dead
of Hiroshima,
of Nagasaki.

We are holding candles: we kneel to set them
afloat on the dark river
as they do
there in Hiroshima. We are invoking

saints and prophets,
heroes and heroines of justice and peace,
to be with us, to help us
stop the torment of our evil dreams . . .

        *

Windthreatened flames bob on the current . . .

They don't get far from shore. But none capsizes
even in the swell of a boat's wake.

The waxy paper cups sheltering them
catch fire. But still the candles
sail their gold downstream.

And still the trees ponder our strange doings, as if
well aware that if we fail,
we fail also for them:
if our resolves and prayers are weak and fail

there will be nothing left of their slow and innocent wisdom,

no roots,
no bole nor branch,

no memory
of shade,
of leaf,

no pollen.

Philip Levine

Then

A solitary apartment house, the last one
before the boulevard ends and a bricked road
winds its slow way out of town. On the third floor
through the dusty windows Karen beholds
the elegant couples walking arm in arm
in the public park. It is Saturday afternoon,
and she is waiting for a particular young man
whose name I cannot now recall, if name
he ever had. She runs the thumb of her left hand
across her finger tips and feels the little tags
of flesh the needle made that morning at work
and wonders if he will feel them. She loves her work,
the unspooling of the wide burgandy ribbons
that tumble across her lap, the delicate laces,
the heavy felts for winter, buried now that spring
is rising in the trees. She recalls a black hat
hidden in a deep drawer in the back of the shop.
She made it in February when the snows piled
as high as her waist, and the river stopped at noon,
and she thought she would die. She had tried it on,
a small, close-fitting cap, almost nothing,
pinned down at front and back. Her hair tumbled
out at the sides in dark rags. When she turned
it around, the black felt cupped her forehead
perfectly, the teal feather trailing out behind,
twin cool jets of flame. Suddenly he is here.
As she goes to the door, the dark hat falls back
into the closed drawer of memory to wait
until the trees are bare and the days shut down

abruptly at five. They touch, cheek to cheek,
and only there, both bodies stiffly arched apart.
As she draws her white gloves on, she can smell
the heat rising from his heavy laundered shirt,
she can almost feel the weight of the iron
hissing across the collar. It's cool out, he says,
cooler than she thinks. There are tiny dots
of perspiration below his hairline. What a day
for strolling in the park! Refusing the chair
by the window, he seems to have no time,
as though this day were passing forever,
although it is barely after two of a late May
afternoon a whole year before the modern era.
Of course she'll take a jacket, she tells him,
of course she was planning to, and she opens her hands,
the fingers spread wide to indicate the enormity
of his folly, for she has on only a blouse,
protection against nothing. In the bedroom
she considers a hat, something dull and proper
as a rebuke, but shaking out her glowing hair
she decides against it. The jacket is there,
the arms spread out on the bed, the arms
of a dressed doll or a soldier at attention
or a boy modelling his first suit, my own arms
when at six I stood beside my sister waiting
to be photographed. She removes her gloves
to feel her balled left hand pass through the silk
of the lining, and then her right, fingers open.
As she buttons herself in, she watches
a slow wind moving through the planted fields
behind the building. She stops and stares.
What was that dark shape she saw a moment
trembling between the sheaves? The sky lowers,
the small fat cypresses by the fields' edge
part, and something is going. Is that the way
she too must take? The world blurs before her eyes

or her sight is failing. I cannot take her hand,
then or now, and lead her to a resting place
where our love matters. She stands frozen
before the twenty-third summer of her life,
someone I know, someone I will always know.

Sharon Libera

How You Were Born

For six years, having no child,
your father and I taped cardboard to our window,
photographed butterflies on Sundays, ate
or did not eat, fought over who would do dishes.

I entertain you with stories. . . .
Our white dog as a pup came home purple —
the next day I found the pokeberry branches.
You say, "That's funny," and ask,
"Was I there?"

I cannot distinguish how you were begun,
except — with thermometer and graphs
you were plotted, and brought pleasure
time after time. Once,
out of doors, awkward on my back
on a mossy rock above a cove in Maine —
but that time did not make you,
though I was sure it would.

In the womb you answered to "Hilary," male
or female, "merry" or "lively."
At the big fight in "Rocky" you wanted out,
but I had to stay,
with one eye on the clock.

LIST MATERIAL YOU WISH TO SEE
(FICTION HAS NO NUMBER)
SEE OVER FOR LOCATION IN LIBRARY

BOOK
NUMBER

PN
11 36. 57

AUTHOR

PS
595

TITLE

IS A SUBSTITUTE BOOK ACCEPTABLE?

YES _____ NO _____

YOUR NAME _____

After a ping like a rubberband,
the bed soaked, I insisted on washing my hair.
Your father, timing my pains,
was shouting over the shower.

Hair wet, the car speeding
between river and mountain —
far down, red and white lights cut off the way.
An ambulance threaded the valley ahead of us.
The girl died in an hour, as if your two souls
traded places.

I woke up frozen from the waist down.
The delivery room was cold, no place to sit.
Your father was bored and had goosebumps.

In another alcove screams began.
Nurses tried over and over
to reach that woman's doctor.

My obstetrician, cool and cynical,
checked me like an oven slow roasting a bird.
At my last visit he said you would be a boy.
I believed him.
In the mirror I saw the melon of your head
stretching me, my boy!

Shiny forceps pried you out
as if I were a can difficult to open.
"It's a nice one, a girl."
In shock, I almost missed you —
held high, squashed forehead, red,
looking most like your father's aunt,
a woman pure of heart but homely.

When they brought you to my breast
we were prepared to look you over
to see what we'd got:
you, staring
into my face, then into your father's,
considering what you had got.

Margo Lockwood

Oxford Street Museum

At eighteen when I worked in Oology,
in the Egg Room on the fifth floor,
stabled above the door that read
Nabokov: Entomology
where we looked at tarantulas
all during lunch—

nature, far from being in me,
or something I was "of,"
was the courtyard I walked down into,

the air a relief from formaldehyde
soaking through the bodies
of the dead animals, mounted
in crowded victorian cases.

Autumn air, or snappy chill snow-speckled
air, or oozing lavendar spring air
was nature or the beginnings of it.

The study that fogged the air deep
inside, was all Latin or Greek to me.
Nomenclature, species-differentiation—

I was a good speller, but that
was it, as far as science went.

Science was a country where I went to work,
as if into a war zone.
My life, however, was another question.
As real as my skin, my hair,
the dynasties of DNA molecules
for which I was the Egg Room.

Health

The post office automatic writing system
I use to communicate with you,
my beloved dead, is getting fogged over.

It used to be I couldn't have
a pencil in my hand
but that words would stain out, onto paper,
elegaic, melancholy.

Now I leave my baggage at home,
and I walk around this city
that I know like my old pair of boots,
too well, the scuffed apparatus of it.

There is a reason for this lightness.
I was starting to notice myself
breathing heavily.
You have moved away from me,
out into the starry worlds, I guess.

Memory is doing its encapsulation trick.
Your faces, the pores of your skin,
the liquidity, the hue of the iris of your eyes,
fade for me and I seek other,
living faces to take my pleasure with.

I make small prayers against unfaithfulness.
I hope, I trust, it is because
you loved, I loved you, well.
To the hilt,
to the bloody hilt,
I sometimes think.

Nail Letter

In the dark, I picked up a nail
to write you a letter
on a piece of wood.

The iron point of midnight will
failed me, I couldn't send it.

I am brave like Joan of Arc
in dreams, but things shrink
back into place when I awake.

There are some tired flowers
here with me, two roses almost
turning back to black,
a flowering quince that drops
its petals everytime I move,
in an old green clay jug
that stands for Ireland.

All the lace in the windows
is like the pointillist lives
that people let one in on.

My favorites are on the north side
of the Liffey, where the windows
are just about exhausted, and the
lace is very old,

I am like a peeping tom
enjoying things that everyone
else ignores or is ashamed of,
the dirty old lace that I know
is valid, as the days gone by are.

One doesn't have to be in a museum
or happy. Sometimes the picturesque
is enough to carry you forward.

Robert Lowell

In the Ward

Ten years older in an hour—

I see your face smile,
your mouth is stepped on without bruising.
You are very frightened by the ward,
your companions were chosen for age;
you are the youngest
and sham-flirt with the nurse—
your chief thought is scheming
the elaborate surprise of your escape.

Being old in good times is worse
than being young in the worst.

Five days
on this grill, this mattress
over nothing—
the wisdom of this sickness
is piously physical,
ripping up memory
to find your future—
old beauties, old masters
who lost their friends before they lost their minds.

Your days are dark,
and night is light—
here the child says:
heaven is a big house
with lots of water and flowers—
you go in in a trunk.

Your feet are wired above your head—

If you could hear the glaring lightbulb
sing
your old modernist classics . . .
They are for a lost audience.

Last year
in buoyant unrest,
you gathered two or three young friends
in the *champagne room*
of your coldwater flat
to explore the pedantry
and daimonic lawlessness
of Arnold Schoenberg
born when music was still imperfect science—
his ever-retreating borderlands of being
that could not console.

If you keep cutting your losses,
you have no loss to cut.

Nothing you see now
can mean anything;
your will is fixed on the lightbulb,
its blinding impassivity
with-holding disquiet—
the art of the possible
that art abhors.

It's an illusion death or technique
can wring the truth from us like water.

What helpless paperishness,
if vocation
is only shouting what we will.

Somewhere your spirit
led the highest life;
all places matched
with that place
come to nothing.

Three Poems for *Kaddish*

Sometime in the early 1960's, Robert Lowell began to collaborate with Leonard Bernstein on Bernstein's third symphony, *Kaddish*. Three poems were written before the collaboration was broken off. Bernstein in the end wrote his own text.

I

Brothers, we glory in this blinding hour,
our loins are quickened by the heat of power,
we think the sun draws nearer day by day.
All creatures now obey
the motions of our uncreating hands.
Our whole world is a Caribbean sea,
we bake our hearts out on the sands.
We worship thee, Oh bathers' sun,
and in our terror ask if Solomon
in all his beauty was arrayed like thee.

God hung the rainbow in the sky,
the sign of his contrition and our peace.
He knew man's self-dominion would increase.
We need no help from Providence to die.

Because we were forgetful of God's ways,
will he rejoice and watch our planet run
like a black coffin round the sun
with frigid repetitions of his praise?

I think our little span has reached its end,
that henceforth only ruin will regard
the breathless planets and the sun descend
aeons around an earth whose crust is hard.

They ask me to sing a song;
I, the lily of Sharon, the rose of the valleys,
I, the wasted!
How can I sing a new song,
rolled stem and blossom
in this strange land?

Can God destroy us in the act of praise?

II

Who understands the fierce intelligence
that gazed upon the ancient world and found
nothing but disease and violence
ruled the imagination of its mind?

The heavens opened and the waters roared,
cities and peoples crashed before the flood.
How shall we sing the praises of the Lord,
who looked upon this work and found it good?

Was God sure
that our extinction was our only cure?

Men saw the heavens' open windows pour
destruction on the land for forty days;
from sun to sun, they filled the earth with praise,
but now we know the Lord of Hosts is poor.

Father, we watch creation's downward curve,
and think the fevers of our sickness shake
your old head, and destroy its inner nerve;
the knotted muscles of your forehead break.

Poor little Father, we have stained your grace,
and heaped our coals of conscience on your head,
and now you hardly dare to show your face,
for in our dying, you are surely sad.

Look in our fallible and foolish glass,
your own face stares at you like withered grass!

III

Winter and darkness settle on the land;
above the river, green, avenging ice
advances and resumes its old command,
our north and south poles hold us in a vise.
The sun has dropped, and there is nothing here
but frozen fishermen whose lanterns burn
above the ice-holes. Listen, you will hear
the saber-tooth and mastodon return,
dazed monarchs of this arctic wilderness,
they rule with shaggy, crushing stubbornness.

The sun has dropped. We listen for a sign:
the manna scattered from God's hand like bread,
a pillar of fire to show our path and shine,
a hero with a rainbow on his head.
No, none of these. The sun has dropped. We must
suffer the silence of the dead machine,
whose self-repairing wheels need no unseen
mechanic, when they grind us into dust.
The system runs on its own steam. The clock-
maker has no surprises for the clock.

Yet still we stand and sing into the cold,
and trust we never can annihilate
the old, established order of the world;
we know that by creating we create.
Poor little Father, are you looking down
on us without volition to resist?
Our hands have turned creation on its head.
Oh Father, do not bite your lip and frown;
it hardly matters now if we made God,
or God made us. Both suffer and exist.

Thomas Lux

On Resumption Of The Military Draft

We only want to count you, boys, to find out who
and where you are. We don't need
a draft. We do need to know where we can find you,
just for the files. I wouldn't worry,
it would be a lottery, and you are lucky.
You might as well go down and sign up now.
You must. We only want to count you, boys.
You can't go to Canada anymore,
we've closed the doors. You wouldn't like prison,
you've heard about what goes on in there.
Listen, even if: you don't have to cut your hair.
Don't forget — *there's no war,* no jungles
and gooks. This time it'll be fair,
especially for the niggers and the poor,
who last time, whining, took their simple losses.
We need to know where we can find you.
You need to find: a post office.
Hell, there's no such things as bayonets
anymore. You never get that close.
Mostly we'd need cooks and clerks, not many medics,
some maintenance — skilled — and if you're chosen
it's good for the country and for you.
You can do what you want but it pays
to go along. We don't *need* a war, you know
that won't happen, we had it
with hootch-lightings, leaves and leaf, leaf, green,
green on green, weren't allowed . . .
It's the way we do it and we know how.
We only want to count you, boys, to find out who and,
though it's unlikely we'll need to know, where you are.

The Hunting

Killing anything was pure accident.
A dumb stalker, a worse shot—I went
almost daily, to the woods.
A favorite prey was slow

and shallow: a brook.
I'd say, as it moved languidly:
Don't move, you rascal! And when it did,
of course, as it does, I'd shoot.
I liked that: no wound,

or at least a wound that healed
instantly. Once, however, a rogue
squirrel came into my scope
and stayed there, like a nut, eating

nuts, for half an hour.
Meaning only to frighten, I aimed about
a foot above and to the left—one shot, dead

between the ears. Thereafter, to guarantee
life, I aimed to kill, and thereafter
never did. I did love and dread

those scraggly woods, particularly
the getting to the center,
where, in snow or summer, I'd sit,
rifle across my knees, waiting

there at the heart of it
for something—silent, armed: a failure
and pleased with my failing.

The Milkman and his Son

For a year he'd collect
the milk bottles—those cracked,
chipped, or with the label's blue
scene of a farm

fading. In winter
they'd load the boxes on a sled
and drag them to the dump

which was lovely then: a white sheet
drawn up, like a joke, over
the face of a sleeper.
As they lob the bottles in

the son begs a trick
and the milkman obliges: tossing
one bottle in a high arc
he shatters it in mid-air

with another. One thousand
astonished splints of glass
falling . . . Again
and again, and damned
if that milkman,

that easy slinger
on the dump's edge (as the drifted
junk tips its hats

of snow) damned if he didn't
hit almost half! Not bad.
Along with gentleness,

and the sane bewilderment
of understanding nothing cruel,
it was a thing he did best.

Derek Mahon

'The World Is Everything That Is The Case'

— Wittgenstein, *Tractatus*

The world is everything that is the case
From the fly giving up in the coal-shed
To the winged Victory of Samothrace.
Give blame, praise, to the fumbling God
Who hides, shame-facedly, His agèd face;
Whose sun retires behind its veil of cloud.

The world, though, is also so much more —
Everything that is the case imaginatively.
Tacitus believed mariners could hear
The sun sinking into the western sea;
And who would question that titanic roar,
The steam rising wherever the edge may be?

Cleopatra Mathis

The Traveler

It's raining like the day you walked out,
harmonica in your pocket, the suitcase of shirts.
I'm thinking of you again, with your variety
of wives: the cajun, my mother the Greek,
and Alberta, the Texas peach.
Reminded by this dull rain and every man I see
absently touching the child, of how you smiled
and left, never sent letters or money.
Consider your ten years to make it back
just that once. My blond-ringleted picture
yellowing inside your wallet, You were so charming,
at ease. To forget, I sliced the length of every finger
with a gillette blade. Now the next wife writes:
you want to be a father. Daddy,
here is my reply, filled with your debts, my deadly slashes
of memory. You left blood behind, that permanent
    traveler
thickening our lives. Do you know
how long it outlasts hate,
love; do you know how long?

William Matthews

Bystanders

When it snowed hard, cars failed
at the hairpin turn above the house.
They'd slur off line and drift
to a ditch — or creep back down,
the driver squinting out from a half-
open door, his hindsight glazed
by snow on the rear window
and cold breath on the mirrors.
Soon he'd be at the house to use
the phone and peer a few feet out
the kitchen window at the black
night and insulating snow.
Those were the uphill cars. One night
a clump of them had gathered
at the turn and I'd gone out
to make my usual remark —
something smug about pride disguised
as something about machines and snow —
and to be in a clump myself. Then
over the hillbrow one mile up the road
came two pale headlights and the whine
of a car doing fifty downhill through
four tufted inches of snow atop a thin
sheet of new ice. That shut us up,
and we turned in thrall, like grass
in wind, to watch the car and all
its people die. Their only chance
would be never to brake, but to let
the force of their folly carry them, as if

it were a law of physics, where it would,
and since the hill was straight until
the hairpin turn, they might make it
that far, and so we unclumped fast
from the turn and its scatter of abandoned cars;
and down the hill it came, the accident.
How beautifully shaped it was, like an arrow,
this violent privation and story
I would have, and it was only beginning.
It must have been going seventy when it
somehow insinuated through the cars
we'd got as far away from as we could,
and it left the road where the road left
a straight downhill line. Halfway
down the Morgans' boulder- and stump-
strewn meadow it clanged and yawed,
one door flew open like a wing, and then
it rolled and tossed in the surf of its last
momentum, and there was no noise from it.
The many I'd imagined in the car were only one.
A woman wiped blood from his crushed
face with a Tampax, though he was dead,
and we stood in the field and stuttered.
Back at the turn two collies barked
at the snow plow with its blue light
mildly turning, at the wrecker, at the police
to whom we told our names and what we saw.
So we began to ravel from the stunned
calm single thing we had become
by not dying, and the county cleared
the turn and everyone went home, and, while
the plow dragged up the slick hill the staunch
clank of its chains, the county cleared the field.

Alice Mattison

Cool Day in July

It's too cold to swim, so you're taking the children
to the fire truck parade in a town somewhere near
the place where you're staying.
Just as you're ready to start, though, an ancient car
pauses to let out a woman with a baby.
It's Anita. "But we didn't even know you were coming—
you might have missed us—"
"Oh, I'd have waited. Maybe I'd have broken in."

You admire the baby, and they get into your car.
You're pleased, but you've been thinking
thoughts she'd laugh at, so you have to fix them,
though she's already teasing (the town
is hidden in the hills): "You're sure you didn't just
wish for a parade?" —but then you find the road, and
as you go, she tells you, abbreviating over the
kids' heads, what's been happening to her.
She was arrested—
passing a bad check.
She claims she didn't do it, but an hour later,
speaking, ostensibly, of someone else,
she almost admits she did.
She will get off— her friend the lawyer is encouraging.
You look at her sitting there, bright-faced, with the baby,
the sleeves of her white shirt
rolled neatly above her elbows.
She'll get off.
The judge, anyway, doesn't know about the drugs.
Or, maybe, these days, she is even off the drugs.

The fire trucks are volunteer companies
from all over that region. The firefighters
have all attempted uniforms, even if only
matching t-shirts.
You are not standing at the best spot.
There is a ceremony you can just hear— diagonally across
        from you
—it is not just fire engines.
The gold-headed cane is being presented to Harry Dacey,
age ninety-four, the oldest inhabitant.
The former oldest inhabitant died this spring.
They've been doing this, it seems, since 1924.
You can see him chatting with the officials,
trying out the cane as if
it just occurred to him—
"Here's what I've been looking for!"
You're surprised he doesn't feel
the way *you'd* feel
if they hauled you out there for one of the things you
don't like to think about.

But the baby is fussing, and your kids are hungry
so you walk toward the car, half-hearing, behind you,
the announcement of other awards,
the voice muffled by trees.
Is it "the fattest inhabitant" he is saying?
and some that are open to transients and
visitors— the person with the funniest fear
(you don't hear it— you're almost at the car—
but it has something to do with watermelon)
and another you can't make out at all, but
—suddenly you hear perfectly— the winner is you.
Of course you pretend you don't hear
but you're sure they are calling your name, several times.
Luckily, the children have run ahead

and Anita is saying, "Why am I like that?
I wish I were more like you, more—
stable." "*Stable*?" you say,
but after lunch you tell her, "It's just that
your oddities
show." She has a ride back,
a nervous man who appears at supper time
in another ancient car, but he
cuddles the baby
and instantly hits it off with your children, who teach him
how to catch a frog, before
they all take off with a bag of fruit for the trip.

Hunter Radiation Center: Halloween

(for Kate)

It's the one thing you've asked for — your medicine *now*, not
hours from now, on the way home, after
this new rigmarole
of your x-rays, tests, upstairs, downstairs —
but I simply can't find a drugstore.
Back at the clinic, I can't even
find *you* again — I'm shown to
still another waiting room.
It's empty. I sit down.

People enter in couples: a man comes in with
a gray-haired woman in a purple poncho. She
crochets yellow yarn.
Then comes a handsome man, curly white hair, and a woman
older than he is. *She's* doing handwork
I've never seen; I think it's tatting.
"Madam!" calls the gentleman. He has the voice
of a Christmas caroler: bracing, sure. "What a
beautiful poncho you're wearing.
Did you make it yourself?"
"Oh, do you like the colors?"
"Blue is my *favorite* color."
I look again; no, there's no blue.
"He's legally blind," says the other man, to me,
"but he even does needlepoint, using a special machine."
"Is that tatting?" I can't help asking.
"Yes, it's tat-ting," says the man with the voice,
pronouncing all the t's.
The woman beside him looks up, and explains that
she is his sister, a widow from Oklahoma.

She says, "widder."
I've never heard that, except in the movies.
She's come for the winter
to see to her brother, and is tatting
bookmarks for Christmas presents. Tatting's
small: easy to slip into a bag.
Everything's colorful: her brother (the patient)
wears a red and white gingham shirt.

There's only one reason to be here.

The elevator door opens; the receptionist
cries out before we can see what's there.
She pushes buttons; nurses appear.
It's a four-year-old girl, brought in by her parents,
dressed as the Easter Bunny. "Betsy!"
Everyone knows her but you and me.
(You've turned up, and are waiting
for your next bout with the machine.
Absently, you finger your chest.
You look like
someone
being interrupted —
still making a point while
turning toward the persistent voice: "Yes? *What?*"
I explain about the drugstore.)
Betsy's parents tell us
that Karen, the radiation therapist,
made the bunny hood.
The rest of the costume's
a pair of pink pajamas.
"Are you going trick-or-treating tonight?"
"Try and stop her." Karen herself
sits down and
takes Betsy onto her lap. "Feel my pockets."
Candy in both of them!
The hood is beautifully made, of pink felt.

You remember the hospital pharmacy.
I find it, after a search; but they don't take
prescriptions intended for the outside.
I'm almost in tears, but you
snatch the prescription and vanish,
bursting in, somewhere, on your doctor, who
writes it up on the other pad.
This time it all works;
I get the medicine, you swallow it,
and you're finally called for your minute behind the door.

The medicine
won't help, nor will the treatment.
You don't even know how to knit.
I do,
but I'm slow — if I started a sweater for you
it wouldn't be
finished in time: and you're so tall, too —
such yards of knitting! "You're *family*," you say,
but I'm not:
my relatives
are short, like me —
I take you in my arms, to
comfort you, but
it is I in yours.

Gail Mazur

Baseball

for John Limon

The game of baseball is not a metaphor
and I know it's not really life.
The chalky green diamond, the lovely
dusty brown lanes I see from airplanes
multiplying around the cities
are only neat playing fields.
Their structure is not the frame
of history carved out of forest,
that is not what I see on my ascent.

And down in the stadium,
the veteran catcher guiding the young
pitcher through the innings, the line
of concentration between them,
that delicate filament is not
like the way you are helping me,
only it reminds me when I strain
for analogies, the way a rookie strains
for perfection, and the veteran,
in his wisdom, seems to promise it,
it glows from his upheld glove,

and the man in front of me
in the grandstand, drinking banana
daiquiris from a thermos,
continuing through a whole dinner
to the aromatic cigar even as our team
is shut out, nearly hitless, he is
not like the farmer that Auden speaks
of in Breughel's Icarus,

or the four inevitable woman-hating
drunkards, yelling hugging
each other, and moving up and down
continuously for more beer

and the young wife trying to understand
what a full count could be
to please her husband happy in
his old dreams, or the little boy
in the Yankees cap already nodding
off to sleep against his father,
program and popcorn memories
sliding into the future,
and the old woman from Lincoln, Maine
screaming at the Yankee slugger
with wounded knees to break his leg

this is not a microcosm,
not even a slice of life

and the terrible slumps,
when the greatest hitter mysteriously
goes hitless for weeks, or
the pitcher's stuff is all junk
who threw like a magician all last month,
or the days when our guys look
like Sennett cops, slipping, bumping
each other, then suddenly, the play
that wasn't humanly possible, the Kid
we know isn't ready for the big leagues,
leaps into the air to catch a ball
that should have gone downtown,
and coming off the field is hugged
and bottom-slapped by the sudden
sorcerers, the winning team

the question of what makes a man
slump when his form, his eye,
his power aren't to blame, this isn't
like the bad luck that hounds us,
and his frustration in the games
not like our deep rage
for disappointing ourselves

the ball park is an artifact,
manicured safe, "scene in an Easter egg,"
and the order of the ball game,
the firm structure with the mystery
of accidents always contained,
not the wild field we wander in,
where I'm trying to recite the rules,
to repeat the statistics of the game,
and the wind keeps carrying my words away

A Deck of Cards

This chorus girl was pensive,
Sadness was on her brow,
Till she met her Sugar Daddy,
And she's ex-pensive now!
                    —from a Varga queen of hearts

When Mister Mulryan called me into his office
to "show me something," I was lucky—
all he flashed was playing cards,
nude women in white cowboy hats,
one with a curving fishing rod and net.
I was eleven, no one could blame me
for confusing sleazy glamor and sex
and keeping it to myself, for finding
a goatish camera salesman romantic.

My father would have fired him
and avoided me for days.

At home, I took to the darkened den
and watched TV, old as I was
for Howdy Doody, and contemptuous
of Big Brother Bob who cursed one day
when he thought the microphone was off.
My father suffered, never to find me
waiting in the hall. The love I wanted
came late at night, after he'd left me
to lie in my spool bed, as my sister
in her spool bed slept the sleep
of someone still a child. Then I met
my 2-dimensional man, nasty in his cowboy hat
and spurs, dangerous with a dangling cigarette.

Only my grandfather saw me change,
watching from the hardship of retirement.
"Hedy Lamarr!" he called me, or "Veronica Lake!"
when my hair fell softly in my face.
Then I looked in the mirror and thought:
"Pretty?" I pretended terrible sore throats,
stayed home from school, wandering voluptuously
from my bed to the overlit bathroom
where I preened with rouge and Shalimar perfume...

The next year I was taller than half
the boys in school. Too awkward suddenly
for baseball with my brother's friends,
I borrowed a canoe and paddled on the Charles
to meet a destiny Thoreau had never
recognized. Sunk from the transcendental
mores of my favorite stories, I floated
on the dirty river, where toughs in rowboats
flirted across the waterlilies. Flattered,
ignorant, I paddled the term away.

In seventh grade, we traded dog-eared
books we didn't read but hid, and peeked at.
My Beginning Latin teacher confiscated one
from me, and blushed. I kept a diary
that Mother couldn't see...

Omnia Gallia in tres partes divisa est.
I was divided, too—what use was Caesar?
I waited for my body's lines to curve,
remembering verses from Mulryan's deck
as I skipped home from school, mouthing
racy words, happy knowing everything is secret—
luscious secrets I'd never learn to keep.

Joe-Anne McLaughlin

Great-Aunt Francesca

"Girl, it's taken everything in me
just to keep myself breathing."

Half then all our chickens
picked off by coyotes, the pig gut
he salted with strychnine,
meant for coyotes, eaten by his own
dogs, the burial of the dogs
useless against the coyotes,
the reburials, the coyote hunters
shooting our goats, his stallion
breaking its leg, startled
by something that looked like
a coyote, the shooting of the stallion
the burning of its carcass
and in the rain, burning, burning,
for days, him taking to mint gin,
turning on me with his shot gun,
that night giving me a hand gun,
locking himself in the storm cellar;
I tell you I ran, ran outrunning
the coyotes, ran and told no one.
Please, please don't ask me anything.

James McMichael

From the McMichael's,
Florence. She passed the Silver's, the Johnson's.
She was walking to Martello and the bus. She was
the woman who took care of me, and she was going
shopping.
It was that one time in her life, a Saturday,
an afternoon. She was alone again. Glen was in
Tobruk, or somewhere, in the army, and it was years
after her first husband died, after the early
photograph in Eaton Canyon with the light
about where it was now. She had posed between
two oaks, the heels of each hand flat against them,
sleeves to her elbows, wind, the canyon to one side
dark at the falls where John Muir climbed and found
wild ferns and lilies, villages of wood-rats.
She'd gone only to the falls and come back out
to Pasadena, and the afternoon was just as late
now as it had been then. The sun was low and almost
blocked by the houses south of other houses
facing that way, as ours did. If she started
home again from downtown through the streets,
the houses that she passed between my room and there
were waiting for new tenants, for the doctor, for a
sober, infirm neighbor of the Hale's to stop
scorching his nose and forelock as he tried to
light his cigarette. If I heard her at the
back door with her packages, I knew that she would
soon start dinner. I'd watch, and she would let me
plead with her about the story of the fire,
give in and tell it, answer what I'd ask.

If I were with her, houses that my father sold
were possible, each at its certain distance from the
vineyard five blocks north. The mountain was absurdly
vertical and dark, and the cars that passed below it
droned in their stupor through the pepper trees.
Stick-piece-place, the stable with the horse and dog
were possible, remembered. Lights were going on in
other kitchens—yours before your parents moved there,
mine at some one time when Florence was with Glen.

How light it was outside was a matter
neither of us thought about. Florence went on
working at the sink. We talked, and I kept
busy with the #20 New Connecticut grinder,
turned the crank and sent the bit along in
spirals, like a barber-pole. I took it apart,
followed its channel with my thumb and fit it
back in place securely with the wing-nut, tight.
I did all that again, each step, and we kept
talking. So that when we heard her car
and looked out past the palm tree to the street,
how light it was above the lawns or shrubs,
how far she'd driven or how far he had to drive
was easy, sure, and as composed as any
look she gave me when she came inside. She
talked with us a little, left us to our
interests in the kitchen. We heard his car
and knew that he was glad to be here, glad
for anything we had to tell him, and for her.
    He knew she'd live five years. She wouldn't
think about it, would be in and out of
wheel-chairs, hospitals, assuming to the end
that she was getting better. That made it
tolerable for her, and covered him to work

so thoroughly at what he did all day
that coming home was easy. Dinner. Florence
leaving. Me in bed, asleep. Alone, it was
their time, unless the phone would ring. It would be
for him, some business matter, and would last
indefinitely while she did something else,
arranged the flowers for a still-life sketch,
wrote letters, read. I tell myself that
how they were with one another was as natural
as any hesitation, as their reluctance
ever to let me walk beyond the Johnson's
or to school. If they were frightened or remote
they lived it over quietly, kept working,
made a long trip up the coast, with me.
I'd go to dinner with them at the Esterbrook's.
To houses that he'd show on weekends with his sign
staked in the front lawn.
          After she died, his business kept him longer.
Florence had moved away with Glen, and I was
there alone through the afternoons and early
evenings, into the hours when I'd listen
to the radio and wait to hear him drive in,
late. After 10, after my shows were over, I'd
worry every way he might be killed, would give it up
only and completely when his car was there.
With that exhilaration I could put on
all the calmness that I thought he wanted—
pretend to be asleep or answer tiredly
that I was there. I was certainly there, and
had been, hadn't been with him, wherever
he had been. But I didn't hate him for it,
loved him with a dull, morose, uncomplicated need
that made his days as strange to me as where he
spent them.

"An Apple Fell in the Night and a Wagon Stopped"

"It comes back to me."
We say that about remembering, as if from
longer ago than we knew we had touch with,
from before we were born and in someone else's life,
"An apple fell in the night and a wagon stopped."
We were asleep then and heard neither. She
herself was asleep. There had been only
night to hear when the ground reported the blunt
fall of an apple. A wagon that had started somewhere
stopped.

James Merrill

Ideas

CHARLES *and* XENIA *are discussing them*
At her place. Interrupted solitaire,
Fern, teapot, humdrum harmonies from where
Blinks a green cat's-eye, the old FM.

XENIA: Now no. But when I am child my parents
Are receiving them. Emigrés I think very old,
Distinguished. Spectacles with rims of gold.
Clothes stained by acid of expérience.

Forever I am mixing them, although
My father explain, this one is physicist,
Archéologue, poet, so, down the list.
Tongues they are speaking sometimes I not know,

But the music! After dinner they are
Performing 18th century trio or septuor
As how do French say digestif before
Mother is bringing out the samovar.

When they have finish tea they kiss, pif paf,
My father's both cheeks and my mother's hand—
Me too, if I go not yet to Dreamland
So late bezaubert on my little pouf.

Maybe I visit Necropole in Queens
By underground with flowers once a year
To show respect. But they are buried here,
Here in my heart. CHARLES: Oh you Europeans . . . !

Mine by comparison are so, well, crude,
Self-pitying, opportunistic, young. Their gall
Is equaled only by that paradoxical
Need for acceptance the poor dears exude.

I'm sitting quietly? Up roars the motorbike
Cavalcade—horns, goggles, farts of flame.
They swagger in as if their very name
Implied a nature seminal, godlike.

One strips. One dials Biloxi. One assumes
The lotus position; and all, that I am who
Was put on earth to entertain them. As I do.
You simply wouldn't believe the state of my rooms,

And the racket, and the 6 x 18 psychedelic
Daubs. One whole spring, I shut my doors to even
The few I fancied. Can you think what heaven
It was not to have to hear the syllables "Tillich,

Hesse, Marcuse," at least not from their lips?
Back they went to the glassy Automat
They thought was the Ritz, before we met.
Just picturing them there, though, their collapse,

Without me, into vacancy, the joint
Stubbed out in ketchup, I began to feel,
Well, sorry. How long since their last real meal?
And was I all that fond of needlepoint?

Besides, the simplest can appear—once dressed
In things of mine, and keeping their mouths shut—
Quite presentable. Not in smart places, but
You know my soft spot for the second best.

Enfin, considering the lives they've led,
They're shaping up. Some of my polish must
Be rubbing off on them. Now if they'd just
Learn to stick to their side of the bed—

Midnight already? I've a date. Bye. *Goes.*
The music stops. XENIA *resumes her Patience.*
VOICE: This performance of the Enigma Variations
Has brought our evening concert to a close.

Paul Muldoon

Cuba

My eldest sister arrived home that morning
In her white muslin evening dress.
'Who the hell do you think you are
Running out to dances in next to nothing?
As though we hadn't enough bother
With the world at war, if not at an end.'
My father was pounding the breakfast-table.

'Those Yankees were touch and go as it was —
If you'd heard Patton in Armagh —
But this Kennedy's nearly an Irishman
So he's not much better than ourselves.
And him with only to say the word.
If you've got anything on your mind
Maybe you should make your peace with God.'

I could hear May from beyond the curtain.
'Bless me, Father, for I have sinned.
I told a lie once, I was disobedient once.
And, Father, a boy touched me once.'
'Tell me, child. Was this touch immodest?
Did he touch your breasts, for example?'
'He brushed against me, Father. Very gently.'

Carol Muske

Real Estate

You think you earned this space on earth,
but look at the gold face of the teen-age
pharaoh, smug as a shriner in his box

with no diploma, a plot flashy enough
for Manhattan. Early death, then what
a task dragging a sofa into the grave,
a couple of floor lamps, the alarm set

for another century. Someday we'll heed
the testament of that paid escort watching
himself in all the ballroom mirrors: Slide

with each slide of the old trombone,
be good to the bald, press up against
the ugly duck-like. Time is never old,

never lies. What a past you'd have
if you'd only admit to it: the real estate
your family dabbled in for generations,
the vacant lots developed like the clan

overbite — through years of sudden
foreclosure. Who knows what it costs?
First you stand for the national anthem,

then you start waltzing around without
strings, reminding yourself of yourself,
expecting to live in that big city
against daddy's admonition: buy land,

get some roots down under those spike
heels, let the river bow and scrape as
it enters the big front door of your property.

Carole Oles

They Set Out in Fog

They're determined to have fun.
The boy's 14 today. He's chosen
this trip North to where they lived
a life before him. There's the attic
in the gray Victorian where pigeons
nested until the cooing wasn't cute.
Where the husband put his fist — why? —
through the wall. The owners' fights
rose through forced-air heating vents.

      At water's edge
a sailboat levitates on mist, seagulls
neither leave nor cease their flight.
All this salt air stings an open past.
At the coffeehouse, they tune in 12
French tourists, discover they can translate
Shall we sit in front or back?
You'll take spiced wine?

      No connective
gets them to the boy's fall in mud
beneath the lighthouse, the father's
accusation. Sealed inside the moving car,
they say the thing which cannot be unsaid,
she flings the car door wide, forcing
him to stop, someone innocent is crying,
earth is flowing in runnels to the sea . . .

Going home
they transport silence. Dark now,
and the rain has gotten dangerous,
too many travelling close and fast.
She thinks of Jeffers at his ocean —
"better for men To be few and live far
apart, where none could infect another."
Beside the highway, lights from houses,
reference points along the night.

She knows today won't end: her father, dead,
comes home reeling every Christmas Eve.
How inscrutable, pronouns in her mother tongue.
She wants to say they love. To say how love,
like all their dreaming, mixes fog and salt.

Veterans Day, 1981

In last week's *New York Times* I read
the First Lady's announcement from the White
House: a joke writer was hired until it all blew
over, the enemy's cheap shots
about expensive gowns and china. Appease
your critics with a laugh, she said. Disarm

them. Meanwhile the paper's full of arms
deals. "Capability" is spread
worldwide like a synonym for peace
and nobody needs to see the whites
of anyone's eyes to fire the shot
heard round the big blue

marble that nobody's left to hear. This blue-
print for disaster went to charm
school. It wouldn't *really* shoot
us out of history, out of the red.
It'd just be a kind of joke to write
till the pressure was off. We'd aim to please.

I remember how my father eased
his grief when FDR died. He blew
three loud blasts into his white
handkerchief, covered his face with his arm
and looked up much later, redder
than sunburn. The shot-

glass came down from the closet and he shot
loss dead. I was too young to be pleased
he cared so much. I only saw that grown man red.
Now I find myself singing the blues
for what I think we've lost and will. I'm alarmed:
when did I last love my leader? White-

washes aside, who wears a white
hat for us? Maybe those who make moonshots,
not arms. I want arms —
these things attached to our shoulders — in their place.
Starting with language, the true blue
chip. Orwell knew. They're worse if we call them "reds".

Bloodshot eyes mean I drink too much red wine while the
      blue sky
darkens. Think of the world silent as a white page where,
      once,
someone with an arm, a hand, could have written *Stop.*
      Please.

Steve Orlen

All That We Try To Do

I had been thinking about love, how hard
It is to remember
How to fall in love,
How love has the frankness
Of giving in and the firmness
Of logic, and yet when I tried
To discover this order
I noticed, far down on the beach,
The swimmers testing
The water, which must have been
Colder than the air
In winter, and I noticed
On the porch below me
The two elderly brothers, my great-uncles,

Staring at the girls on the boardwalk
And, when the sun was right,
At boats sailing on the sea beyond.
Up in my shared rented room
Behind the window
I could remember my love
For a girl fifteen years ago
In summer: light through the trees
On her black hair
As she knelt beside me
Having just done something she
Didn't know people did, even in love.
The effect would last

For many years, though we never married,
The prickly shy girl
And the boy who did not know what
To say about love
So he spit
At a horse dragging a wagon
Of tomatoes and eggs past his house.
I remembered wanting to make
Another kind of love with her,
Not to the body,
But to whatever rose
Quietly out of us.

When I looked up again
Three teenage girls
In bikinis and sneakers
Were teasing the brothers. The girls'
Poor postures
Accentuated their breasts.
My great-uncles
Must have been thinking
Something, though they
Neither moved nor spoke.
Each had a daughter
And a son with children who drove
To this beach on weekends from their jobs.
The girl I was thinking about
Had a mouth too perfect
So she rarely spoke.
That wasn't it, of course,
But that's what I thought
And all that we thought or did,

All that we tried to do to love
Each other, what difference
Has it made? As though seeing the swimmers

In the cold water
And the uncles staring from the porch,
As though remembering that girl
I loved such a long time ago
Calmed me so much
Life could be generalized.
But what? The boardwalk, the teenagers,
The old horse
And the driver who yelled
To-ma-toes! Ai-igs! When
Was it too late
To fall in love? I wasn't even listening.

Linda Pastan

Family Scene: Mid-Twentieth Century

In the photograph you and I sit together
with identical smiles,
each holding a dog by the collar;
the ocean is simply backdrop.
Marriage, could be the caption,
which frees and confines at the same time,
as those leashless dogs, now dead,
were checked by our hands on their collars.
It is probably just coincidence
that I found this photograph pressed
between pages of Tolstoy, though
I always said that you looked Russian —
Pierre, I suppose, not Vronsky, with your passion
for land and for growing.
Someone will find this picture
years from now and think:
mid-twentieth century, family scene,
people had pets instead of children.
Though of course we had children too
off somewhere, swimming perhaps
in that backdrop of water.
Who were we smiling for, ten years ago,
and what can we believe
if not our own faces in photos?
When you want to go faster, go slower!
a poet said, speaking of running marathons.
I want to go slower now, seeing only
darkness ahead, but you always hurry me on.
Didn't you rush us into our life together,

almost without thinking,
or at least holding our thoughts
the way we might hold our breath?
And didn't it all work out? you ask,
for there we are, twenty years into our marathon
caught in black and white and smiling,
and here we are now.
Dumb luck, my father would have said,
who never quite approved of you.
But who can ask for anything more of life
than those strategies of the genes
or the weather that we call luck?

Joyce Peseroff

The Hardness Scale

Diamonds are forever so I gave you quartz
which is #7 on the hardness scale
and it's hard enough to get to know anybody these days
if only to scratch the surface
and quartz will scratch six other mineral surfaces:
it will scratch glass
it will scratch gold
it will even
scratch your eyes out one morning—you can't be
too careful.
Diamonds are industrial so I bought
a ring of topaz
which is #8 on the hardness scale.
I wear it on my right hand, the way it was
supposed to be, right? No tears and fewer regrets
for reasons smooth and clear as glass. Topaz will
                    scratch glass,
it will scratch your quartz,
and all your radio crystals. You'll have to be silent
the rest of your days
not to mention your nights. Not to mention
the night you ran away very drunk very
very drunk and you tried to cross the border
but couldn't make it across the lake.
Stirring up geysers with the oars you drove the red canoe
in circles, tried to pole it but
your left hand didn't know
what the right hand was doing.
You fell asleep
and let everyone know it when you woke up.

In a gin-soaked morning (hair of the dog) you went
hunting for geese,
shot three lake trout in violation of the game laws,
told me to clean them and that
my eyes were bright as sapphires
which is #9 on the hardness scale.
A sapphire will cut a pearl
it will cut stainess steel
it will cut vinyl and mylar and will probably
cut a record this fall
to be released on an obscure label known only to
aficionados.
I will buy a copy.
I may buy you a copy
depending on how your tastes have changed.
I will buy copies for my friends
we'll get a new needle,
a diamond needle,
which is #10 on the hardness scale
and will cut anything.
It will cut wood and mortar,
plaster and iron,
it will cut the sapphires in my eyes and I will bleed
blind as 4 A.M. in the subways when even degenerates
are dreaming, blind as the time
you shot up the room with a new hunting rifle
blind drunk
as you were.
You were #11 on the hardness scale
later that night
apologetic as
you worked your way up
slowly from the knees
and you worked your way down
from the open-throated blouse.
Diamonds are forever so I give you softer things.

The Long March

The Rabbi saw a Torah-scroll
surrounded by a fence with one picket
missing...The iron points glowed,
and the gap was like a missing tooth
in the face of God. *So Talmud was written.*

I let the book slide to the floor, and shred
puckers on the pink chenille bedspread.
This is my new aunt's room. She's away
for her only year at college...A week before,
she bought a pair of stuffed Scotty dogs
and gave one to her best friend. "That one is Dip,
and mine is Loma." But then
she didn't want to take it with her...

I've shut the door
against Grandma and Phil. No gaps in the fence!

Carol's book has pictures,
and a song the False Messiah sang to himself,
imagining how it would be:
      "Messiahs, Messiahs, many wish to see—
      But above all others
      Stands Shabati Zevi..."

Carol paints. She showed me a picture she called,
"Almost perfect. It's just this part I couldn't get right."
The canvas is full of color, like confetti.
The corner she couldn't get right is grey and empty.

Loma has a black button nose...and a beanie
with slits for his perky ears.
Grandma got rid of Taffy when she married...
The new super didn't allow pets—not even canaries!

I miss the Chevrolet sign that flashed in the sky
on rainy nights like lightning. I thought, that's what
the Northern Lights must be. The Northern Lights,
Disneyland,
the seven rings of Saturn,
and the blue grotto of Capri—all far away
as Grandma's old hallway
with floors like tiles I'd seen in the Museum:
CAVE CANUM. (A volcano covered them.)

Robert Pinsky

The Figured Wheel

The figured wheel rolls through shopping malls and
    prisons,
Over farms, small and immense, and the rotten little
    downtowns.
Covered with symbols, it mills everything alive and grinds
The remains of the dead in the cemeteries, in unmarked
    graves and oceans.

Sluiced by salt water and fresh, by pure and contaminated
    rivers,
By snow and sand, it separates and recombines all droplets
    and grains,
Even the infinite sub-atomic particles crushed under the
    illustrated,
Varying treads of its wide circumferential track.

Spraying flecks of tar and molten rock it rumbles
Through the Antarctic station of American sailors and
    technicians,
And shakes the floors and windows of whorehouses for
    diggers and smelters
From Bethany, Pennsylvania to a practically nameless,
    semi-penal New Town

In the mineral-rich tundra of the Soviet northernmost
    settlements.
Artists illuminate it with pictures and incised mottoes

Taken from the Ten-Thousand Stories and the Register of
  True Dramas.
They hang it with colored ribbons and with bells of many
  pitches.

With paints and chisels and moving lights they record
On its rotating surface the elegant and terrifying doings
Of the inhabitants of the Hundred Pantheons of major
  Gods
Disposed in iconographic stations at hub, spoke and
  concentric bands,

And also the grotesque demi-Gods, Hopi gargoyles and Ibo
  dryads.
They cover it with wind-chimes and electronic instruments
That vibrate as it rolls to make an all-but-unthinkable
  music,
So that the wheel hums and rings as it turns through the
  births of stars

And through the dead-world of bomb, fireblast and fallout
Where only a few doomed races of insects fumble in the
  smoking grasses.
It is Jesus oblivious to hurt turning to give words to the
  unrighteous,
And is also Gogol's feeding pig that without knowing it eats
  a baby chick

And goes on feeding. It is the empty armor of My Cid,
  clattering
Into the arrows of the credulous unbelievers, a metal suit
Like the lost astronaut revolving with his useless umbilicus
Through the cold streams, neither energy nor matter, that
  agitate

The cold, cyclical dark, turning and returning.
Even in the scorched and frozen world of the dead after the
    holocaust
The wheel as it turns goes on accreting ornaments.
Scientists and artists festoon it from the grave with brilliant

Toys and messages, jokes and zodiacs, tragedies conceived
From among the dreams of the unemployed and the
    pampered,
The listless and the tortured. It is hung with devices
By dead masters who have survived by reducing themselves
    magically

To tiny organisms, to wisps of matter, crumbs of soil,
Bits of dry skin, microscopic flakes, which is why they are
    called "great,"
In their humility that goes on celebrating the turning
Of the wheel as it rolls unrelentingly over

A cow plodding through car-traffic on a street in Iasi,
And over the haunts of Robert Pinsky's mother and father
And wife and children and his sweet self
Which he hereby unwillingly and inexpertly gives up,
    because it is

There, figured and pre-figured in the nothing-transfiguring
    wheel.

The Beach Women

In the fierce peak of the day it's quietly they wade
With spread arms into the blue breakers rushing white
And swim seemingly with no tension, the arms
Curved, the head's gestures circular and slow.

They walk dripping back into the air
Of nineteen-fifty-five smiling downward from the glare
As if modestly, as they move daintily over the sand
Shaking their hair, tingling, taking it easy.

The beach flushes and broils, shapes ripple
In the waves of heat over it and the cold sea-water
Dries on their arms and legs and their suits, too,
Drying out stretched over their bottoms

In the luxury of sun flowering everywhere. The delicate
Salt glazing their skin they dissolve in oil.
Holiday colors throb on suits, towels, blankets,
Footwear, loose robes, bottles, carriers of straw,

Bright magazines and books, gear feminine and abundant,
The whole overwhelming with a sense less of sex than
    gender,
The great oval blanks of their sunglasses hypnotic,
Flashing anonymous glamour over their cards, books or
    gossip.

It was Irving Stone they read, John O'Hara or Herman
    Wouk
Or the decade's muse of adultery: Grace Metallious.
With her picture in *Time,* floppy dungarees, no bra,
Retrospectively a seer, a social critic—

No doubt the cabana boys weren't always lying
About their own ladies, mistresses whose husbands
Came down from New York to tip big on the week-end—
Like Mrs. F, strawberry-blond Italian. . . .

What did she carry down to the sand all summer
But Wouk's *Caine Mutiny,* the earnest young sailors
Behaving like so many Jews, coming over guilty
Because they hadn't let Hitler as Lloyd Nolan

Played by Joe McCarthy send them under the waves.
Good for Grace, writing about "lust" with her flat
Characters and her big breasts. What did Mrs. F
Sunning at the shore fifteen years ago, or anyone,

Think about Caryl Chessman, Chaplin, Lucky Luciano,
Ike and the Rosenbergs? What can I recall? Women,
Moving in the sparkle of the sidewalk, blinding
Even in the reverse colors of the afterimage

Outside the drugstore where I worked, no cabana
        Lancelot,
Grateful for a wet cuddle with a chubby majorette.
I made club sandwiches and Sundaes, on dark dark days
        purveyed
Dozens of copies of *Confidential:* "Victor Mature

"Locked Me In A Cage" and "Russ Tamblyn's All Girl
        Party"
Cheered them up while the rain slashed gray
Soaking the boardwalk and gleaming on cars.
On those days I admired their tans, white dresses

And pink oval fingernails on brown hands, and sold them
Perfume and lipstick, aspirins, throat lozenges and Tums,
Tampax, newspapers and paperback books—brave stays
Against boredom, discomfort, death and old age.

Robert Polito

Spring Training

Dear Bob:

Thanks for your typical douche letter.
Since Xmas I haven't been doing much.
I can say that I'm not watching
TV all day, or smoking pot. I read
Books, write letters, learn Swahili,
—Smoke pot—, look for jobs, which
Includes travelling and throwing my knife.
I'm getting pretty good at it.
I can, once in the groove, throw my knife
From 15 feet or so with killing force.
The next step is 22 feet.

I bought a young black racer.
Normally this kind of snake doesn't
Do too well in captivity.
I handled her every day and I thought
She had become quite tame. I remember
When she put her head in my mouth.
But about 3 weeks ago, just after
I left for Florida, she escaped.
Now she is at large, —somewhere
In the house. I wish she had cobra
Venom and would bite my motherly hag.

I'm not going to dwell on the tryout,
But I failed. I went down
To the Mets' Spring Training Camp

In St. Pete. They gave me
A real Mets uniform, and treated me nicely.
I threw about 50 pitches—
My curve wasn't working but I felt
My fastball was 90% effective.
After my workout the head
Of the entire Mets Farm System
Sat me down and began telling me
How, while I was in good shape
And had pitched "alright,"
I just wasn't good enough. He said
They have guys 3 or 4 years younger
Who can throw just as well.
I still have a tryout with the Orioles
But my mind isn't on baseball
Like it used to be. Even though
I failed, I felt a sense of liberation—
I got this "baseball doubt" out of my system,
Or at least into perspective.

Ping-pong is now my game.
I try to play as much as possible.
Gary is pretty well occupied
With Nancy and beer.
Billy can't get out here enough.
I met this kid who's just as good.
We've had some great games.
I think I'll be getting a job soon.
Once I have a job, I think
I'll be spending much of my free time
In Philly at the table tennis club.
Billy and I went over to check it out—
They've got some great looking players
And equipment at this place.
The club has eight excellent tables.
It costs $25.00 a month — which ain't bad.

If I can play there enough
I can become quite good . . .
I can't wait for our upcoming battles.

The job I'm pursuing most is police work.
Nobody is hiring. But I was up
In Harrisburg talking with a good friend
Of my father who was a State Patrolman
For 26 years. He seems to think there may be
An opening on a rural township PD.
That would be perfect — working
As a cop in the Pennsylvania countryside.
I want to carry a machine gun.

Good luck with acupuncture.
I talked to your mom a week ago
To find out when you were coming home.
She didn't seem too keen on the idea,
But I think there's mucho truth
In this oriental practice.

I'm not going to tackle your spiritual
Activities. It's up to each of us
Either to pick it up or ignore it.
I don't think one can go wrong
Getting into spiritual activities,
However. I don't remember you
Putting my thoughts down last Xmas,
Though. But maybe I don't remember
Your criticisms as unsound . . .
I hope you continue your evangelical
Ways when we get together again.

Keep in touch—

Love,

First Love

The day's too beautiful;
The Spring sun on the porch too warm . . .
He's restless; nothing can contain him —
Not his books, or a whole house full of toys,
Not even the hidden fortress he's built
Deep in his grandmother's garden —

For this is his special day.
His secret love is coming to have dinner
With his parents, *with him* —
Irish, plump, black hair
Set like a helmet over her red face;
An old student of his mother's dead sister,
Smelling of soap and flowers,
He can't wait to see what she's brought him,
Can't wait for her soft words, her wet kiss . . .

So he decides to meet her car.
First, he skips to the corner of the street,
And waits . . . A half-hour seems to go by
But still no sign of her great black Chrysler;
He thinks he knows her route,
Recalling the day she drove them to her house,
And slowly he sets off, one street at a time,
Stopping at each new corner to look all around —
Down the street they take to Mass,
With its wall of trim, brown three-deckers;
Along a wide avenue, divided by a strip of land
Where there are benches and trees;
Then he's not so sure where he is anymore —
Suddenly there's what looks like a highway;
So he starts walking in the other direction,

Trying to retrace his steps,
But it's all new to him, unfamiliar.
He keeps walking until he's too tired to go on,
And humiliated, lonely,
He sits down on another porch, and begins to cry.

He's certain he'll never see his parents again,
Never see Barbara,
When a minister he mistakes for a priest
Comes out of the house, and saves him.
He brings him inside, asks his name,
And goes to the phone;
Returning, he says, "They sound like nice people.
You know they've been very worried about you."

The minister's wife, and their two grown daughters,
Make much of him — they sit him in the sun,
Stop his crying, wash his face,
And feed him soda and cake.
He can't remember ever being treated so nice —
He feels like the young prince in one of his story books.

But at last there's her black car —
Once again in tears, he runs to them,
To Barbara, to his mother and father,
Telling them over and over
That he didn't run away, that he loves them,
That all he wanted to do was *meet her car* —

His mother's crying, and Barbara,
They hug him, and say they're glad to have him back . . .
His father too —
                    But suddenly *he* seems confused;
He pulls his son away from the two women,
And starts to shake him —
                    "Do you understand

How much trouble you've caused us?
Do you know that you walked *over five miles?*
That's one for every year of your life" —

He seems about to hit him;
Anger and awe alternate on his face —
                                                    Just like the time
The boy received his first tool box,
And went off by himself for an entire afternoon,
And patiently, methodically,
Sawed the railing off the back porch —
His father furious,
But amazed that he could do that with a toy saw —

Anger and awe crisscrossing his face,
Like crosshatching,
Or like those cheap prints
Where the rabbit becomes a duck,
And the beautiful girl turns into a skull grinning from ear
        to ear;
His awe equal to his anger —
So that in the end he's unable to strike.

Katha Pollitt

In Horse Latitudes

(*—The Horse Latitudes are a region of unusual calm, lying in the North Atlantic Ocean. When sailing ships were becalmed there, the crew used to throw overboard cargo and horses. Thus lightened, the boat could take advantage of whatever wind there might be.*)

What does the sea want, my clothes, my keys, my face?
This is the mind's Sargasso,
Expansive as Kansas flatlands, the big dead place.

The weeds stir, they make promises; I'm light as a shell.
Immobile, the sea bottom
Glints at my emptiness with ship's tackle, jewels,

Railway tickets, photographs: the blue-eyed platoons
Grinning up from their doomed jungles.
I am left with nothing to hold, nothing to do

But imagine those horses the Spaniards abandoned here:
At night I have seen them rise
To graze the glassy prairie and whinny their fear.

Anxious, disconsolate,
They sniff for a wind. Sour water drips down their tails.
Ghost horses, I am like you: when the gray line of a sail

Threads the horizon, my heart strains forward too:
Heavy with salt, the blood,
Leans like a tide, but has no place to go.

Cathleen Quirk

No Dead Ends

Don't ever hold on to anything!
Let it go! Let it go!

And you've got it.
— *Claire*

"Don't lay your trip on me, ladies.
I don't care if you've got a headache, a muscle
hurts, your old man has split with another chick,
or what your dreams are...

Drop your shoulder! Stop leading with your neck!
Like quit trying to *protect* yourself. Just keep
that *standing leg conscious!* Your eyes! Your eyes!
They're dead in your head. When you do movements,
always work against yourself—you push down

to get up. Now, throw yourself out into space
and *perch* there. Send your spine right out of your head!

This movement is a figure 8, the double planes keep coming
one after the other...so find the spiral in you
and hook it up with all the other spirals happening.
It's a simple problem, like 4. You deal
with fours all day long. But you'll never find your *center*

until you push through in the hips. That's it,
push through in the hips. You're all locked up in
yourself...Unjam! Stop looking like you're humming
to yourself. Like, there are no dead ends in movement...
the end must always suggest another beginning.

And another thing, ladies. In *twenty five
years,* I never left a class before it was over.
Even that time I had to sit on the radiator. . .
sucking lemons I was so nauseated.

Ladies, dancers don't have periods."

Michael Reck

Once More O Ye Etc.

In what heaven or hell
do you, Bob, booze?
If heaven, there's gin
sempiternal, you wake on a cloud
press a button
and an angel comes in
with an enchanting tinkle

or, if you're allowed
in the Elysian Fields
(why not? you
boozed an epic amount),
you'll wander till
you find that stream
of gin, of gin, more gin

and life eternal
will be one colossal
binge, you'll tell
your odd little stories
in that phony accent
and the angels will clap
and everyone will dance

or if hell (semblable, frère)
you'll roll forever
liver caved in,
crying for the pain,
crying because you're afraid
crying for the one
thing that consoles you, gin.

Kenneth Rexroth

Marichi

An hour before sunrise,
The moon low in the East,
Soon it will pass the sun.
The Morning Star hangs like a
Lamp, beside the crescent,
Above the greying horizon.
The air warm, perfumed,
An unseasonably warm,
Rainy Autumn, nevertheless
The leaves turn color, contour
By contour down the mountains.
I watch the wavering,
Coiling of the smoke of a
Stick of temple incense in
The rays of my reading lamp.
Moonlight appears my wall
As though I raised it by
Incantation. I go out
Into the wooded garden
And walk, nude, except for my
Sandals, through light and dark banded
Like a field of sleeping tigers.
Our racoons watch me from the
Walnut tree, the opossums
Glide out of sight under the
Woodpile. My dog Ch'ing is asleep.
So is the cat. I am alone
In the stillness before the
First birds wake. The night creatures
Have all gone to sleep. Blackness

Looms at the end of the garden
An impenetrable cube.
A ray of the Morning Star
Pierces a shaft of moon filled mist.
A naked girl takes form
And comes toward me — translucent,
Her body made of infinite
Whirling points of light, each one
A galaxy, like clouds of
Fireflies beyond numbering.
Through them, star and moon
Still glisten faintly. She comes
To me on imperceptibly
Drifting air, and touches me
On the shoulder with a hand
Softer than silk. She says
"Lover, do you know what Heart
You have possessed?"
Before I can answer, her
Body flows into mine, each
Corpuscle of light merges
with a corpuscle of blood or flesh.
As we become one the world
Vanishes. My self vanishes.
I am dispossessed, only
An abyss without limits.
Only dark oblivion
Of sense and mind in an
Illimitable Void.
Infinitely away burns
A minute red point to which
I move or which moves to me.
Time fades away. Motion is
Not motion. Space becomes Void.
A ruby fire fills all being.
It opens, not like a gate,
Like hands in prayer that unclasp

And close around me.
Then nothing. All senses ceased.
No awareness, nothing,
Only another kind of knowing
Of an all encompassing
Love that has consumed all being.
Time has had a stop.
Space is gone.
Grasping and consequence
Never existed
The aeons have fallen away.
Suddenly I am standing
In my garden, nude, bathed in
The hot brilliance of the new
Risen sun — star and crescent gone into light.

Michael Ryan

Why

I wish I could walk deep into a field
of spiked wheat reaching my waist
and not ask that question,
where the sun laces my chest
with its indifferent heat, and the sky
seems only a backdrop for sharp birds
that tuck their wings and glide,
where each step pops crickets into quick arcs
like bingo balls in the glass air machine
an old man sits to watch at evening
and does not ask that question
of himself, or of anyone near him.

Because *why* can land you in prison.
Why can walk you to a traffic island
where you find yourself for no reason.
Why can enter your dreams like a demon
and you wake up the next morning
not the same.
        It always starts this way,
breeding inside until it swarms into things,
blackening the sky, in chorus with wind . . .

Tonight, in summer, cornered in my room,
jamming my hard feelings into a wordless song
that has hummed for centuries snagged in the genes
and now pokes out of my particular brain
into these words, taut as a thorn,
and demands a brief life of its own,

so, too, I want to be done
lugging through the gloom,
and wish I could walk deep into a field,
stretch out my joined limbs, and hold on.

———

Conscious in darkness, the lost thoughts
almost heard, like whispering in the distance:
I click off my light, watch the pines
sway with their own weight—
huge furred arms motioning *come on*
with the swish and caress of black waves.

Who has not watched the ocean at night
and heard its old invitation?
That same dusky word licks through the pines.
I press my face against the screen
and remember I did this exact thing
as a child on my grandmother's farm
waking one night to roam the house alone.
There was something out there I didn't know,
in the shadows, under the deep black trees,
something that wanted me. I wouldn't go to it
for anything, but suddenly even the house
seemed strange, and I felt it touch me
all over like cold air after a shower.
Afraid, I squeezed behind the ancient radio
and spent the night. It became a family joke.

Was there a moment then I could have known
why the world shoves us away while taking us in?
That question needles my brain like a germ.

———

Who gives a shit about carcajou
in the boscage, or pansies freaked with jet?
I'd like to write a daylight song,
to pretend the world's a good friend,
but what relation to things makes a link
that won't snap with all the shaking it gets?

In this thick dark the room seems blank
as a man long dead and forgotten.
I can't stop the draining of the days.
But when night edges in, and bad panics hum
like light-drunk bugs diving at the screen,
it still brings sweet expectations of return.

And what pleasure comes just lying in the sun,
or talking intensely, or loving someone—
what pleasure enters, private as a dream,
rushing through the body from the slightest thing,
through the nooks and caverns, bouncing like sound,
until it fades to whispers, and then it's gone.

Outside, the great pines face a black sky.
What can be named that is close and stays?
I know the silence of an empty house
can greet at the door with an amazing smack.
I don't want to hear what keeps me apart
when I whirl my one dance toward the large.

———

What first word first rounded out a mouth?
And what dumb animal spoke it?

Like a child who sings himself to sleep
the brain turns to itself at night
because the delicious burnish of things
melts into the dark.

So now I write
about loneliness, how it pockets me inside it,
and the longing to be freed from it
I always walk around with.

It doesn't matter that now it's summer
and the breeze might let me forget
if I could lie here naked and blank,
because breeze comes easy as a sexless kiss
and breeze won't plant me finally
outside myself, and that is what I want.

Still it pleases me to think of you
reading this in another time and place,
at another chance axis of those old infinites,
while I sit in this green chair in Massachusetts,
while I think even at this moment we orbit,
even at this moment we wave past
with a faceless prehistoric minding-our-business
which is neither desperate nor malicious,
like two similiar beasts at a brief distance
when the whole world was a forest.

Where I'll Be Good

Wanting leads to worse than oddity.
The bones creak like bamboo in wind,
and strain toward a better life outside the body,
the life everything has that isn't human.

Feel the chair under you? What does it want?
Does lust bend it silly like a rubber crutch?
Tell a tree about the silky clasp of cunt.
It won't shift an inch. It won't ache to touch.

Let me not cruise for teens in a red sports car,
or glare too long at what bubbles their clothes.
Let me never hustle file clerks in a bar.
Keep me from the beach when the hot wind blows.

If I must go mad, let it be dignified.
Lock me up where I'll feel like wood,
where wanting can't send me flopping outside,
where my bones will shut up, where I'll be good.

Andrew Salkey

Drifting

For whom do I speak, now,
so far away from home?
For whom do I write, now,
so far away from myself?

I speak for the experience
of the flux I've become;
I write for the concrete
to fill in the distances

from the house on the road
I lived on, from the warm
home on the sea I crossed,
from old voices to the new.

And I suppose that's true,
to some extent, of shipping
oneself far away from port,
finding oneself while drifting.

Gjertrud Schnackenberg

Holding a Raccoon's Jaw

Snow melting when I left you, and I took
This fragile jaw we'd found in melting snow
Two springs before I left, beside a brook
Where raccoons washed their hands. And this, I know,

Is that raccoon we'd watched for every day.
Though at the time her wild human hand
Had gestured inexplicably, I say
Her meaning now is more than I can stand.

We've reasons, we have reasons, so we say,
For giving love, and for withholding it.
I who would love must marvel at the way
I know aloneness when I'm holding it,

Know near and far as words for live and die,
Know distance, as I'm trying to draw near,
Growing immense, and know, but don't know why,
Things seen up close enlarge, then disappear.

Tonight this small room seems too huge to cross.
And my life is that looming kind of place.
Here, left with this alone, and at a loss,
I hold an alien and vacant face

Which shrinks away, and yet is magnified —
More so than I seem able to explain.
Tonight the giant galaxies outside
Are tiny, tiny on my windowpane.

Lloyd Schwartz

Who's on First?

"You can be so inconsiderate."
                              "You are too sensitive."
"Then why don't you take my feelings into consideration?"
                                                  "If you
weren't so sensitive it wouldn't matter."

                    •

"You seem to really care about me only when you want me
to do something for you."
                    "You do too much for people."

                    •

"I thought you were going home because you were too
tired to go with me to a bar."
                    "I was. But Norman didn't
want to come here alone."

                    •

"I'm awfully tired. Do you mind taking the subway home?"
                                        (*Silence.*)
"You could stay over . . ."
                    (*Silence.*)
"I'll take you home."
                    (*Silence.*)

                    •

"Why do we have sex only when you want to?"
"Because you want to have sex all the time."

•

"Relationships work when two people equally desire to give to each other."
"Relationships rarely work."

•

"Do you love me?"
"Of course—; but I resent it."

•

"Why aren't you more affectionate?"
"I am."

•

"Couldn't we ever speak to each other without irony?"
"Sure."

•

"I love you, you know."
"Yes . . . but why?"

•

"Do you resent my advice?"
"Yes. Especially because you're usually right."

•

"Why do you like these paintings?"
                              "What isn't there is
more important than what is."

•

"Your taste sometimes seems strange to me."
                              "I'm a Philistine."
"A real Philistine would never admit it."
                              "I suppose you're right."

•

"Aren't you interested in what I care about?"
                              "Yes. But not now."

•

"We should be more open with each other."
                              "Yes."
"Shall we talk things over?"
                    "What is there to say?"

•

"Are you ever going to cut down on your smoking?"
                              "It's
all right—I don't inhale."

•

"Sometimes I get very annoyed with you."
                              "The world is annoying."

•

"Your cynicism is too easy."
                    "Words interfere with the
expression of complex realities."

●

"Do you enjoy suffering?"
                    "You can't work if you don't suffer."
"But we suffer anyway."
                    "I know."

●

"Do you think we ever learn anything?"
                                        "I've learned to
do without."

●

"You're always so negative."
                    "I feel death all the time."
"Are you afraid of anything?"
                    "Not working."

●

"What shall we do for dinner?"
                    "It doesn't matter—
whatever you'd like."

●

"Why don't you care more?"
                    "I do."

The Recital

He sits there, staring into the keyboard—
baggy rented tux; sagging shoulders; limp hair
nearly brushing the keys—
                  hesitating to begin.

His eyes glazed, as if he'd been up a week
on Coca Cola and pills;
                  a Coke bottle (giant-size)
half-empty at the foot of the piano bench . . .

A few Music people; secretaries from
his lab; the two poets he had studied with;
and assorted friends
                  half-fill the small hall.

The recital is ambitious, demanding:
Romantic-ecstatic and jagged-Modern—sometimes
hard to tell apart in his playing;

frustrated by the almost willful refusal
of his fingers to deal with all the notes;

but riveting—certain that music has to "intend,"
and stopping at nothing
                  to intend *something* . . .

Encouraging applause: a crooked, self-
deprecating bow from the waist.

Intermission is a relief.

"Amazing piano playing . . . for a physicist."
"Why does he *do* this to himself?"
                                    "He didn't
look happy . . ."
                    "What if he decides to play
the first half over again?"

Back inside, the conversational hum drops;
then grows . . .
                    Where is he? Still backstage?
Home? Dead? . . . The speculation is amused;

and dismayed.

Messages are sent; assurances returned.
Forty, fifty minutes . . . Nobody leaves;

no one is surprised.

Could he have done *anything* to
keep his suffering from the audience?

(How many in it had already
suffered with him his poems, jobs, addictions?)

Or is this his way of trying?

Sheepishly, he reappears . . . And begins.
No waiting.
                    His intensity—this time—
controlled by his intentions . . .

What does he have to go through—;
what process, *effort*, finally
allows him to go on?

And what defeats it?

He'd have a poem accepted by a national magazine,
using an image drawn from his experiments,—
only to withdraw it, out of fear he'd lose his job.

He'd change jobs. Move home.
And give up practicing; virtually
stop writing.

Then cancer . . . springing (he was sure)
from all the pills: making him go through
a surgical attempt to prolong his life . . .

He wanted time
to straighten himself out; to try to write more poems—

he had three months.

Dead before forty,
what brought him distinction

besides what already had?

       His astonishing diversity
       of unfulfilled talent;

       and the unrewarded
       diversity of his suffering.

Jane Shore

The Russian Doll

after Elder Olson

Six inches tall, the Russian doll
stands like a wooden bowling pin.
On her painted head, a red babushka
melts into her shawl and scarlet
peasant dress, and spreading over that,
the creamy lacquer of her apron.
A hairline crack fractures the equator
of her copious belly,
that when twisted and pulled apart,
reveals a second doll inside her,
exactly alike, but smaller,
with a blue babushka and matching dress
and the identical crack circling her middle.

Did Fabergé fashion a doll like her
for a Czar's daughter? Hers would be
more elaborate, of course, and not a toy—
emerald eyes, twenty-four carat hair—
a cousin to mine, but with filigreed petticoats
like a chanterelle's gills blown inside-out.
An almost invisible fault-line
would undermine her waist,
and a platinum button that springs her body open.

Now I have two dolls: mother and daughter.
Inside the daughter, a third doll is waiting.
She has the same face,
the same figure,
the same fault she can't seem to correct.

Inside her solitary shell, that echo chamber
where her duplicate selves are breathing,
she can't be sure
whose heart is beating, whose ears
are hearing her own heart beat.

Each doll breaks into
a northern and a southern hemisphere.
I line them up in descending order,
careful to match the bottom halves
with the proper heads, the heads eye-level
with the wombs — a clean split,
for once, between the body and the mind.
A fourth head rises over the rim
of the third doll's waist,
an egg cup in which her descendants grow
in concentric circles.

Until last, at last, the two littlest dolls,
too wobbly to stand upright,
are cradled in her cavity as if waiting to be born.
Like two dried beans, they rattle inside her,
twin faces painted in cruder detail,
bearing the family resemblance
and the same, unmistakable design.

The line of succession stops here.
I can pluck them from her belly like a surgeon,
thus making the choice between fullness
and emptiness; the way our planet, itself,
is rooted in repetitions, formal reductions,
the whole and its fractions.
Generations of women emptying themselves
like one-celled animals, each reproducing,
apparently, without a mate.

I thought the first, the largest, doll
contained nothing but herself,
but I was wrong.
I assumed that she was young
because I could not read her face.
Is she the oldest in this matriarchy—
holding within her hollow each daughter's
daughter? Or, the youngest—
carrying the embryo of the old woman
she will become. Is she an onion
all the way through? Or maybe,
like memory shedding its skin,
she remembers all the way back

to when her body broke open for the first time,
to the child of twelve who fits inside her still;
who has yet to discover that self,
always hidden, who grows and shrinks,
who multiplies and divides.

The Other Woman

In the first dream she is the enemy—
spangled in love's armor, wearing
the sweater she knitted for him,
and she looks prettier than in the photo

you discover in his bottom drawer
that puts her in perspective—
all scowls and squinting at the sun,
unflattering, as he has captured her.

Possession is nine-tenths of the law.
The dream's percentages are never fair,
reminding you how comfortably she fits
within the familiar outline his body

shapes around her; her face partially
hidden by his, they are laughing at something
private, because your mind still must admit
to the old alliance. In time you dream her

exactly the way you want to see her,
ugly, and one night you catch them
making love in the back seat
of the car you are driving.

For once you think you are in control,
but you must keep one eye on the road
and not swerve from your original fidelity,
while in the rear-view mirror, they sink

below your line of vision. How did you
maneuver yourself into this position?
— as earlier, safe in your single bed,
your parents' night-cries woke you,

and, locking you out of intimacy,
they more deeply locked you in.
In the next dream, with teeth and nails,
tearing at her placid face, you awake

surprised at your capacity for violence,
how good it feels. And you shift
into higher gear. You're driving
through a blizzard and she's beside you,

strapping herself in. Crazy, that your dream
should place a seat belt so conveniently,
and she, compliant as a test-car dummy.
Crazy, how misery loves the company inside us

even when we'd be better off alone.
You make a U turn and invite her home.
Climbing the stairs, the two of you
reenter the battlefield of your bedroom.

Compatriots now, on the double bed,
you ask what she intends to do, now
that she is almost ready to let him go,
but she's not herself, not the woman

in the photo, and by now you've forgotten
what brought you two together —
oh, here he is again, shouting up
through the floor for you both to pay

attention. He slams the porch door shut.
From your window, the red arc
of his sleeve is the last of him you see.
He revs the engine, and aiming the car

at the foundation of the house,
he ploughs into the snowbank below you.
Backs up and ploughs again.
And nothing you can do can make him stop.

Charles Simic

On Pretext

A child was taught
To be a gravedigger.

Pail and plastic shovel
Waiting on the meadow.

Don't leave for tomorrow
What you can do today!

A bit of daylight still left
Among the evening configurations.

With his stooped shoulders
He looks employed in the obvious way:

Dark, damp clods of earth flying . . .

They ought to call him in by now:

The carrot-haired little girl
In the hen-house,

Her sister at the salt-lick.

Dimly Outlined by a Police Artist

An especially forlorn specimen
Answers a marriage ad
On a street of compulsory misfortune
One drizzly November afternoon

Sorrow with its sidekicks and damsels
In a diningroom with a pianola which the subway
      rattles from time to time
A cup of tea with her eyelash floating in it
Cakes the size and color of a little finger
      caught in a door

There's also her grandfather's saber
And the story of how an angel of death
Snatched her purse
On the way home from the evening Mass

Strictly Bucolic

Are these mellifluous sheep,
And these the meadows made twice-melliferous by their
  bleating?
Is that the famous mechanical wind-up shepherd
Who comes with instructions and service manual?

This must be the regulation white fleece
Bleached and starched,
And we could be posing for our first communion pictures,
Except for the nasty horns.

I am beginning to think this might be
The Angelic Breeders Association's
Millennial Company Picnic (all expenses paid),
With a few large black dogs as special guests.

These dogs serve as ushers and usherettes.
They're always studying the rules,
The exigencies of proper deportment
When they're not reading Theocritus,

Or wagging their tails at the approach of
Theodora. Or is it Theodosius? Or even Theodoric?
They're theomorfic, of course. They theologize.
Theogony is their favorite. They also love theomachy.

Now they hand out the blue ribbons.
Ah, there's one for everyone!
Plus the cauldrons of stinking cabbage and boiled turnips
Which don't figure in this idyll.

Tom Sleigh

Hope

For Aunt Hope

Overhung by evergreen, your house was cool
Those afternoons the sun's long ghost shimmered
In the fading curtains. The rocker's senile
Back and forth wore ruts in the floor, the boards'

Soft creaking wheezing in, out. It's seven years
Since I saw you last for the last time,
Your eyes molten with remembrance's flicker
As events like magma poured and cooled, time

Confounding my grown-up face with your image
Of the photogenic, faded child.
Who was I to you? your bed barred like a cage,
A stainless-steel cradle, as in your head

My name roamed connectionless. And you too
Were strange, your hip smashed, your legs drawn up
And shrunken like a cricket's, your eyes' blue
Like clouded water in which I saw trapped,

Lost in terminal helplessness, the eyes
Of my aunt of childhood, ironic, clear,
And merciless, their killing-with-kindness
Stare that sent me to the boneyard hour after hour

Those endless afternoon wars at dominoes
Still lurking aloof from your stranger's face.
I held your hand and saw in the window
The two of us suspended beyond the glass

As through us waved a dusty branch, a rag
Of green wiping our smudge of color
From the air....Seven years, and your name still drags
Its luminous syllable like a lure

My heart still swallows, open-mouthed and hungry,
Its barb of light irresistible:
"Go fish in the boneyard," I hear you say,
Your eyes poker-faced, impenetrable.

Elk at Black Fork Canyon

Great furred noses nuzzling at haybales,
Sidling jaws grinding the sweet
Green fodder, they looked up
To where I hunched, clutching

My coat tighter
As the cold like a mouth
Spoke promises.
Their eyes dark and wary

Stared through me as through crystal
And I dissolved into their looking
Like salt the long, liverish tongues
Licked from the block.

Staring from their eyes,
I bulked like a boulder,
A man-thing carved
Into the stone of the morning—

The mountain loomed into my eyes
Like a monstrous word
Pulverizing in its gutturals
The dwindling pebble

Of my name shouted down
The canyon. Trapped in the stillness,
The boulder-humped meadow, I heard
With more than, less than human ears

The cold mouth of the outdoors
Whisper me my wish:
Bone-trees sprouted
In mossy symmetry, skin

Coarsened with velvet fur,
And jaw and nose elongated
And snuffed the freezing air
With the cold scrutiny of a connoiseur.

My smell no longer wrinkled their nostrils
Or set their ears flapping, foolish,
But still lordly. Wholly animal,
My heart rose on knobbled

Legs lunging and stumbling
In the thicket of my chest
To the wild forebears, their heads lifting
Crowns of antlers as if kings —

Bursting in my ears, my name
Crashed back from the stillness
As beneath the unshod
Hooves the snow-crust

Cracked with frigid speed,
The wheeling, flicking tails
Unsheathed like skinning-knives.
They shyed off down the canyon,

Disappeared into the beard
Of fog lengthening down the mountain,
The trampled snow spattered
Golden from their urine.

W.D. Snodgrass

A Valediction

Since his sharp sight has taught you
To think your own thoughts and to see
What cramped horizons my arms brought you,
   Turn then and go free,

Unlimited, your own
Forever. Let your vision be
In your own interests; you've outgrown
   All need for tyranny.

May his clear views save you
From those shrewd, undermining powers
That hold you close just to enslave you
   In some such love as ours.

May this new love leave you
Your own being; may your bright rebirth
Prove treacherous, change then and deceive you
   Never on this earth.

Now that you've seen how mindless
Our long ties were, I pray you never
Find, all your life through, such a blindness
   As we two shared together.

My dark design's exposed
Since his tongue opened up your eyelids;
May no one ever lip them closed
   So cunningly as I did.

Liz Socolow

Taint

Did your mother ever wear a hat
with a whole bird's nest growing on it,
or a dress patterned with naked bodies?
Remember how long the street seemed then,
how you stepped behind her to investigate
a fence post, shop window, blade of grass,
anything to let you fall behind?
Perhaps she was an immigrant, incontinent
even on the street, or especially then,
with a harsh accent when she came
to pick you up from school. You tried
with your eyes, a certain tense breathiness
in your voice to will her dry, silent
in front of your friends. But she *would*
talk, ask how your day went, if your new
sweater kept you warm, if you liked the lunch.
Beneath her the concrete was spotted
on the brightest days. If she worked,
successful, she was always late to plays
in which you had a minor part. Even in her absence
she made you stand out like a new skyscraper
on a bare lot where tenements once stood.

There are moments for wishing to be rubble,
close to the ground, bits of plaster,
chips of brick heaped in a pile of no-color
with one's fellows. Terrible at those times
to meet in the hallway a guest entering
the same party in inappropriate clothes.

The hair is too short or too finely tended.
She chatters immediately familiar in your ear
of her children, her schedule, the thunderstorm
last Monday. Her rings are the size of walnuts
and perhaps you've known her for years,
loved her despite her conservative politics,
her too-wide nostrils, shrill voice. But you care
about the strangers beyond the door and
when you care you always find you are with this woman
though you are grown now, entering a dread gathering
of people who will take the natural cast-away
as your chosen companion for life. You become
small-minded. You shrink to the schoolyard. The fenceposts
are above your head and your eyes scan the tiles
of the hallway for a blade of grass, an abandoned
nest, your mother—anything to keep you back.
While she, flamboyant, in her timidity
punches the doorbell and summons the important host.

The Laughing Angel: Reims

In all the cathedrals of Europe
I've seen only one smiling angel,
feathered wings like the others,
blasted by war. She's famous
not only because she's smiling
but because of the smile.
It might be that the harvest
is fine, but I don't think so:
too much reflected mischief
in her face. As if a gargoyle
had just taken aim with
his spigot-mouth and hit her
exactly where he meant, though
the lines around her eyes
are more joyous, less amused
than that. As if she is watching
how a woman on the way to market
courts a man with invention,
how she puts down her basket
to pick a straw off his back,
another from his hair, small
hay from his shoulders, neck.
It is hard to tell if anything
is there, if they have come
together on the way or will
seal it here to go slowly home;
maybe both. With each catch
of her fingers, the woman
laughs more boldly and he smiles,
the man, he joins the laughter,
in Springtime when the wind
carries no abundance
of dry grass.

Marcia Southwick

The Train Wreck

When it snows after a train wreck,
I like the people to crawl out
and celebrate a little,
to think about winter.

I like it when they open
their battered suitcases and dedicate
some clothing to the wind,

or when they build a fire
and huddle around it,
singing . . .

Why should they know
things could be changed—

a carriage instead of a train,
rain instead of snow,
umbrellas instead of clothing—

or that I've added
an empty train station ahead,
with a cold wind inside
rattling the open windows . . .

When they begin to dance,
the snow still falling around them,
I don't want them to know;

this is the kind
of snow that never melts.

Solo

There are times that falter
like flowers in front of me,
and times that take root in my chest
like a change of heart.
Certain kinds of foliage respond to me.
Ferns, for example, are onlookers.
There are also flowers that have died,
only to be born again like old opinions.
Perhaps it's true that my body
won't always travel solo
away from the place of my birth.
I have come a long way
through the serious underbrush
and will probably come to a clearing soon.
I can't help thinking, though,
of all the shadows I've left behind
and that were once very important to me.
It would be useless to look for them now,
the way it would be useless to keep track
of my footsteps lost in the grass.
And though I would like to be grass,
which doesn't defend itself
but simply waits to become undeniably green,
I know that there is nothing to negotiate.
The old roads that used to lead somewhere
are now overgrown with weeds.
And the sun aches to occupy everything.

Finches

I am a word
in a foreign language —
Margaret Atwood

I am a word in a foreign language,
but I don't know what the word is,
so I sit here quietly,
an alien to my name.
Around me, the hedges rustle.
Finches settle on the roof,
unaware that nothing has changed,
that the field has been plowed again,
holding the seeds inside it like a secret.
And if there were a secret to be told,
it would be my name in another language,
uttered like a prayer for rain,
the rain that is falling beyond me
in another country, the clouds drifting
toward another year.
Now the finches scatter all at once.
There *is* a connection
between myself and their cries:
If bird cries, or shadows,
or too many barns on a hillside
are confusion,
then maybe I should continue
to live in confusion.
But now it's as if the dusk
doesn't have meaning anymore.
And my future is like a weed
that pushes through the same bitter dirt
year after year.

Barry Spacks

Nursing Home

My mother babbles. A salad of noises:
"You know who this is?" asks my aunt and I dread
some horror of an answer, but no,
nothing. She rubs her tray instead.
"It's clean," says my aunt, "the tray is clean.
Evelyn, what are you cleaning? Play
with your cards, play *pishy-posh*," and then she
laughs, that overflowing, tilts
her head at the word and laughs who sits
all day in her chair with her cards in a sweater
embroidered with flowers, all day each day
where the t.v. flickers. My aunt thinks she chose
senility. My aunt says you have to keep
moving, never worry, avoid
abiding mourning,
things that refuse to change.

Counting the Losses

for Helen Corsa

All that is lost is the body
and the object of desire.

Approaching composition, the laureate
said and resaid his name like the clack
of British Railways: *Tennyson,*
Tennyson-Tennyson, murmuring
of innumerable *be*'s—mere being,
humiliating history.

Heinreich Schliemann, final hero
of Troy, once saw as a child a tombstone:
''Here Lies Heinreich Schliemann''—a brother,
dead in infancy—''Beloved
Son'' *himself! in the grave!* He told
lies to the Turks, would have killed to continue
digging for Helen's balconies,
for Priam's gate; a lifetime raising
the other from the dead. That all

we suffer be raised and opened, that
is our portion, work, to lift from the grave—

He who digs is the living son.

All that is lost is the body.

Maura Stanton

The Cuckoo Clock

Before I could tell time, I'd sit and wait
For the cuckoo in my mother's wooden clock
To open his red door, and sing "cuckoo."
I never knew how many times he'd sing,
But the song was regular, and a long trill
Gave me a chance to look inside his house
Where it was dark and smelled of sweet pine.
I used to wonder what he did in there
Under the curlicues of his painted roof.
I guessed he had a parlor, and two chairs
Pulled up before a real brick fireplace.
He drank tea from thin, china cups,
Smeared honey on his crackers, wiped his beak,
And thought of ways he might invite me in.
Though I was large, I was his favorite.
There was no other reason to appear
So often in our kitchen, where the noise
Of younger brothers rose against my ears.
But I couldn't shrink. Too soon I knew
How long an hour lasted, and I climbed
Up on a kitchen chair and pulled the door
Open before it was time for him to sing.
I saw the mechanism, how he fitted
Neatly on his spring above the gear wheel;
And afterwards he ordered me to bed,
Insisted on time for play and homework.
Then yesterday, standing across the street
From my own house, a grown-up clapboard house,
I had the dizzy feeling that I'd shrunk.

This was the cuckoo's house, though I was forty.
I looked at the red door and the pretty trim.
I was small enough to enter, turn the knob,
Sit down in the other chair before his fire,
Sink back, and rest. Why did I hesitate?
I waited on the curb while cars roared past.
I stared at my door, dismissing fancy,
Then went inside to my familiar rooms.
The fireplace was cold, the tea unmade.
I walked around on rugs and oak floors,
And finally paused before the cuckoo clock
Which hung in my dining room — the same clock,
A gift from my mother. It had not ticked
For ten years. The iron chains hung still
Beneath the faded, intricate facade
Coated with fine dust. I put my finger
On the door. I wondered if he heard me.
His lintel was so low. And was his floor
A mess of rubble, dirt, feathers and hair?
I heard him stirring somewhere in the dark
Preparing to greet me, his beak open
Not to sing, but to swallow me at last.

Bathroom Walls

A woman sobs on the toilet.
Hearing her through the wall,
I imagine the pink lace
unraveled from her nightgown
as she strokes her knees.
Upstairs there's a pop.
I suppose a retired barber
spread lather on a balloon
to test his swollen hands;
now he'll hang himself.
No, perhaps two teenagers
shyly undressing for love
with their backs to the mirror
each blew a final bubble.
Somewhere I hear glass breaking.
Of course it's the barber's
bifocals shattered in the sink
as he ties rope to a pipe.
Or is it the teenage girl
who smashed her mirror,
tossing her head in passion,
so that glass fragments fall
over her breasts in facets,
dazzling her lover's eyes
one moment before she bleeds?
You see, I think a man sleeps
downstairs in the bathtub;
when he hears my footsteps,
he thinks I'm someone,
like his grandmother, who darns
socks in her bathroom all night

because the light's brightest.
In his dream I stitch water.
In my dream drops accumulate
until his head goes under.

George Starbuck

Amazing Gracious Living On I-93

I've read the propaganda,
and I believe it now.
I shoulda bought a van de-
signed to squush a cow.
Small cars are "unforgiving."
They crumple up like foam.
It takes a heap o' mortgage
To have a heap o' home,
and if a heap o' heap'll
satisfy some people,
then who am I to holler?

They musta paid top dollar
to furnish a machine
for live-in demolition
derby competition
with stained-glass picture windshield
and Playboy Magazine
entablature. I mean
my little thirteen-inch-wheeled
Rabbit must feel queer
to find me stopping here
to contemplate the roadside
without a HoJo's near.

I mean I've got some odes I'd
like to finish yet
before I make another
bunny silhouette
along the fuselage
of someone's ten-ton Taj
Mahalmobile. Good brother
that comes a little steep.
I like this highway shoulder.
Just sittin'. Gittin' older.
I like it a whole heap.

Stephen Tapscott

Hank

Because he sometimes bored himself with thought
my father taught himself things. Or because
he was an American man, and back from Saipan,
married early, stuck in a stupid job
for the kids, and farm-chores after that.
Or it may have been a kind of silent booze,
he was so silent: sitting in the chair
in his room, which we were not to enter,
in the tobacco penumbra that smelled of hickory
and circled him slowly, marbelling the light

of the upright lamp beside him, he read
for years. I remember *The History of Flight,*
Imitatio Christi, the photographs
of Chinese bronzes Mother wrapped
for Christmas, that went into his room
and kept him there, evenings, for a week.
Then for a while it was the law, *constructs*
he said, and *distinctions.* And then anatomy:
Stubbs on horses first — the stronger fact —
then Gray on human bodies. I turned

my eyes off when he tried to show me, once.
Which was why, I guess, he kept a skeleton
on a hook-stand near him, dried and wired whole.
Momma refused to dust it; no-one said
when he got it, or how, or why, or from whom.
I knew only that it smiled above
behind him, that he told me it was nothing

to fear, that he called it his friend "Hank."
I stood by his chair and looked up, then.
And how I came to be

there I do not remember, in the daytime
when my father was at work, and across
the pale oak floor the varnished light
made the room feel hollow. I was just there,
and a little lonely. I watched it—I mean,
him—because his face was turned away
and he could not see me. As I looked up
from the thighbones I could see the light
pass through his ribs, the dark bars shaped
by open spaces, like the keys on our piano.

If I wanted, then, to lift his hand
and set it on my shoulder, and feel
the white quiet weight of the truth
touch me once, through my tee-shirt....well, I held
back, being a boy. He looked away,
Hank. How he knew it was a man I never
did understand, the man in my father's secret
study; though I supposed there were ways
to decipher such puzzling things. Even then.
Even so long dead and clean of the flesh.

James Tate

The Wild Cheese

A head of cheese raised by wolves
or mushrooms
recently rolled into
the village, it
could neither talk nor
walk upright.

Small snarling boys ran
circles around it;
and just as they began
throwing stones, the Mayor
appeared and dispersed them.

He took the poor ignorant
head of cheese home,
and his wife scrubbed it
all afternoon before
cutting it with a knife
and serving it after dinner.

The guests were delighted
and exclaimed far into the night,
"That certainly was a wild cheese!"

Paint 'Til You Faint

House, house, go away, you're looking
prettier all the time and look me
I'm a rag, a brush, a mop, a hammer.
I'm your lowly employee not what I intended—
I wanted shelter, a self-propelled houseboat.

Housepainting for a fortnight now,
I have no idea how long I've been stroking
white up down back forth when I
slapped a good juicy one across my face—
I can't get mad at a fool like that.

I kept painting as if nothing happened,
I was in a hurry to get to the fine work
so I painted an ant and then I wrote my name
across the forehead of a flea—
anything domestic like this truly enervates me.

Cash-monster, Time-monster, Thought-police.
I keep painting, I would paint the milkman
but he is already painted. I'd like to get
my brush inside that mole-hole—the boob
who sold me this bill-of-goods.

The neighbors have witnessed my devotion
to this busted cesspool of a castle, and now
I am a deacon in the Church of their values—
Silently, silently, we have painted ourselves
into this little plot of earth.

Jelka Revisited

Jelka's profile decorates the doorway to my secret
    architecture.
Jelka's profile chaffs at its own imposture, and the
    indirection
of its stardust infiltrates my polar brain: Welcome
to the material world where omens of the after-world are
    leaked,
flowing like a black shirt. Mountains migrate into my
    head:
I was there to witness the vulgar radiance of her method,
dimly brooding under my Western lamp, accustomed, as I
    am,
to a miscellany of risible phantasms, fatigue never set in.
"Pungent nit, come in! Comfort my belligerent lashes,
    help me
cast out my throes." Jelka's profile, O the asymmetry of it
    all!
She staggers now, and attempts to install a puzzle in her
    smile.
To the tune of Gylfi's mocking, this goddess of illusion
I shall never forget: all living is forgiving. Her profile.

Within Jelka's radius, a Colonel is pulling a thorn
from a comrade's melancholy frown.
There is undischarged thunder in the air. Skeptical,
Jelka looks around, spots a mathematician
playing marbles in the darkened parlor.
Several travelers appear indisposed and refuse
an offer of dinner. Jelka is stimulated

by these companions and walks around
feeling pregnant. Was Hirshvogel going North
or South? "Go after him when you are bigger,"
said the neighbor. The buttons, the buttonholes,
silver heels — brooch which consists of a single
flaming beryl — whisk broom, please, carhop. The fete
by the tomb was a horrible idea. Jelka's tongue
felt like suede. Her slippers, too, were antique, blessed
        things
making sure she "never fell off Mister Floor."

Thirty olive trees are scribbling with crayons
on the bowler hats of eagles — ah, the train!
Jelka snatched up the idle boy, the viscous child saint,
and cuddled him all the way to Illinois.
Wanderers. Whoosh, their luggage. They stand there,
pigheaded in Poisonville, bleeding lemonade
onto the drip-dry tarmac. They are traveling
under pseudonyms, their whole lives flickering
in corridors. Around five, the bonfires,
and they come whipcracking out of their comas.
Lynxes are burrowing into their sleep-filled wagons.
And the boy with the mark of the beast . . . his
transitory gleam and headlong flight . . . Jelka follows him
flattening her endearments against the linoleum
shadow-stippled in the afternoon.

Jelka was lost forever, her costume found burnt
at daybreak. Could have been the city itself
just having a good time. I wish I knew
its name, brute nebulae. When her Collected Phonecalls
were published last Fall, she didn't remember
making any of them. So. American roués.
She was a ghost at her own birthday party.
"Look at her," said the Colonel, "She twiddles the dust-
        babies,

baleful and bluish, with fewer fingernails to grow.
Her life swings back and forth like a tongueless bell,
so far from anyone's home." I wrung his neck, and now
all of that old world is torn down. A coach arrives
to take her back to her inkspot, her uncomfortable

decomposing zones.

Eleanor Ross Taylor

The Painted Bridge

It didn't seem like history. Seemed, more
expediency. . . .

I'm walking to the beauty shop. On Rugby Road
a fractured fume of sodden leaf
and Phi Delts' pizza lunch, and through the pane
one of their rout, white-coated, hands behind,
waits unattending in the wings, waits out
the weary midday to the robust night.

With harness creak of shoulder bag
I mount the railroad bridge, its college news
furled to the wall: day-in-and-day-out cries
in sky blue headlines on pea green BLANK DUKE;
blood red on U-Haul orange overnight
CONGRATS TO SHIRLEY MARILYN
ON PREMIERE OPENING.
                          A starchy stroke
whitewashes smut   then BE HEALTHY LOVE A NURSE
A PHI NOMINAL YEAR AT U-V-A
and JJ as a bare rug (pink on gray).
I null it out.

A tomtom pulsing shakes the maple heads:
below me down the track the train comes on
its big light blazing midday head-on course.
I've never in my life till now crossed when
a train was passing.

                    A striped-capped head
leans out the cab, an arm thrown all-out up
waves wildly.

— Never seen a woman cross a bridge before? —
His eager face ignites at happenstance, but
I hang fire.
                    And suffocating fumes
engulf the wavy birthday caps,
his carpe diem's capped by captioned bridge —
he's under.

                I descend the railroad street.

Below the bridge the blue-lined buckets and
caked lids, the wares the news was made of,
litter the ditch's glittering careless depth.

I'm off. Off for my — *set*.

New Dust

Who was Athena's pet—
Be glad you're dead.
That you should see the shadow fleshen!
The shade caught in the arachnid net—

This dust was Randall and they say
That almost on his lucky day
He found his only luck to be
The dark concrete of 53

I was Athena's pet . . . .
Send me my jeweled bridle,
My Austrian sweater and more books . . . .
Shaking off rejected Anteia
I soared again
Freed of that heaviness.
I watched her fall into the human stars
What gods would take her part?
She said they did . . . .
I wander in the Plain of Wandering
In October, in full light of Pegasus
Having repulsed the lady's love,
Black man in blackness.

(My hoofs strike sparks from you—
I collect them in a basket
For my daughter.
Empty the shelves!
I flew my library to Baltimore
And ate it.)

TO THE 15 BYPASS . . .
    To be fifteen!
    Sabertooth at the Joint Library,
    Gnawing Fannie's knee . . . .
    Here by the laboring highway
    With painful hands I strain . . .
    With a bottle, but no spoon . . . .
    —"Let *that* be a medicine to you."
    (I tell you it sure helps
    To have some sympathy)

I draw towards HWY. 29.
Cars pass—to—
To Greensboro— that's home—
Lucy— and supper . . . .
    A cruel cold snap.
    Not blackberry winter—
    Winter! and a white beard.
    Lost, those vernal altitudes,
    Clambering
    Past my last equinox.

    There was a time, I drove.
    (For the sin of surpassing
    They turned on him—
    The gods, the mount he rode.)

        But what if the story had been different?

    Mother said I had her eyes.
    What I'd give for my own! . . .

This dread is too dreadful

A car has two eyes
A windshield two faces
　　For me, one unflowering autumn
　　It went so ill that I

Two heads two headlights CAR

　　Oh mother
　　I've broken one of my immortal bones
　　blind
　　my immortal I

Henry Taylor

Landscape with Tractor

How would it be if you took yourself off
to a house set well back from a dirt road,
with, say, three acres of grass bounded
by road, driveway, and vegetable garden?

Spring and summer you would mow the field,
not down to lawn, but with a bushhog,
every six weeks or so, just often enough
to give grass a chance, and keep weeds down.

And one day — call it August, hot, a storm
recently past, things green and growing a bit,
and you're mowing, with half your mind
on something you'd rather be doing, or did once.

Three rounds, and then on the straight
alongside the road, maybe three swaths in
from where you are now, you glimpse it. People
will toss all kinds of crap from their cars.

It's a clothing-store dummy, for God's sake.
Another two rounds, and you'll have to stop,
contend with it, at least pull it off to one side.
You keep going. Two rounds more, then down

off the tractor, and Christ! Not a dummy, a corpse.
The field tilts, whirls, then steadies as you run.
Telephone. Sirens. Two local doctors use pitchforks
to turn the body, some four days dead, and ripening.

And the cause of death no mystery: two bullet holes
in the breast of a well-dressed black woman
in perhaps her mid-thirties. They wrap her,
take her away. You take the rest of the day off.

Next day, you go back to the field, having
to mow over the damp dent in the tall grass
where bluebottle flies are still swirling,
but the bushhog disperses them, and all traces.

Weeks pass. You hear at the post office
that no one comes forward to say who she was.
Brought out from the city, they guess, and dumped
like a bag of beer cans. She was someone,

and now is no one, buried or burned
or dissected; but gone. And I ask you
again, how would it be? To go on with your life,
putting gas in the tractor, keeping down thistles,

and seeing, each time you pass that spot,
the form in the grass, the bright yellow skirt,
black shoes, the thing not quite like a face
whose gaze blasted past you at nothing

when the doctors heaved her over? To wonder,
from now on, what dope deal, betrayal,
or innocent refusal, brought her here,
and to know she will stay in that field till you die?

Richard Tillinghast

Things Past

Ten years into memory, a house
  in the bright fluid
time—dark grain of walnut,
  dark
women's bodies, flower-shadows
  in paintings by sisters.

1632 Walnut Street:
  the solid multiples of eight
    like a vintage Oldsmobile,
the curves of the numbers,
  the porch, its roof,
    the porch light
shaped a little by memory—
  lit up like a jukebox,
or an oldfashioned sunset.

Wood doves murmur in the eaves
  as we wake.
Leaf-shadows   sun-circles
  glide over the white ceiling
    from outside our lives.
Xoe's German Shepherd, "Hussah,"
  lolls sheeplike
among the garden weeds.

On the white terrace
Ruthie brushes out her thick hair
  straight and blonde

Between storms   January sunlight
    rare cloud-rainbows
        the air like a telescope
trained on the rain-wet Berkeley hills.

Sisters, Maurya and Tamara,
    your voices! your names!
Mexican smoke curls
    over the drifting walnut grain.

I drive by the house in the rain tonight
    and see myself at the kitchen table.
As I write,
    my notebook rests on an open cookbook.
My beard curls
    in the steamy air
of Christmas turkey soup they are cooking.

Janis Joplin still sings   *Love
    is like a ball and chain!*
The guitar solo cuts through the years
like a pulsating river of acid.

They're drinking coffee together,
    and talking about the past
    that squally, blowsy Berkeley night.
I can hardly see myself
    for the steam gathering on the glass.

Mona Van Duyn

Letters From a Father

1.
Ulcerated tooth keeps me awake, there is
such pain, would have to go to the hospital to have
it pulled or would bleed to death from the blood thinners,
but can't leave Mother, she falls and forgets her salve
and her tranquilizers, her ankles swell so and her bowels
are so bad, she almost had a stoppage and sometimes
what she passes is green as grass. There are big holes
in my thigh where my leg brace buckles the size of dimes.
My head pounds from the high pressure. It is awful
not to be able to get out, and I fell in the bathroom
and the girl could hardly get me up at all.
Sure thought my back was broken, it will be next time.
Prostate is bad and heart has given out,
feel bloated after supper. Have made my peace
because am just plain done for and have no doubt
that the Lord will come any day with my release.
You say you enjoy your feeder, I don't see why
you want to spend good money on grain for birds
and you say you have a hundred sparrows, I'd buy
poison and get rid of their diseases and turds.

2.
We enjoyed your visit, it was nice of you to bring
the feeder but a terrible waste of your money
for that big bag of feed since we won't be living
more than a few weeks longer. We can see
them good from where we sit, big ones and little ones

but you know when I farmed I used to like to hunt
and we had many a good meal from pigeons
and quail and pheasant but these birds won't
be good for nothing and are dirty to have so near
the house. Mother likes the redbirds though.
My bad knee is so sore and I can't hardly hear
and Mother says she is hoarse from yelling but I know
it's too late for a hearing aid. I belch up all the time
and have a sour mouth and of course with my heart
it's no use to go to a doctor. Mother is the same.
Has a scab she thinks is going to turn to a wart.

3.
The birds are eating and fighting, Ha! Ha! All shapes
and colors and sizes coming out of our woods
but we don't know what they are. Your Mother hopes
you can send us a kind of book that tells about birds.
There is one the folks called snowbirds, they eat on the
                    ground,
we had the girl sprinkle extra there, but say,
they eat something awful. I sent the girl to town
to buy some more feed, she had to go anyway.

4.
Almost called you on the telephone
but it costs so much to call thought better write.
Say, the funniest thing is happening, one
day we had so many birds and they fight
and get excited at their feed you know
and it's really something to watch and two or three
flew right at us and crashed into our window
and bang, poor little things knocked themselves silly.
They come to after while on the ground and flew away.
And they been doing that. We felt awful
and didn't know what to do but the other day
a lady from our Church drove out to call
and a little bird knocked itself out while she sat

and she brought it in her hands right into the house,
it looked like dead. It had a kind of hat
of feathers sticking up on its head, kind of rose
or pinky color, don't know what kind it was,
and I petted it and it come to life right there
in her hands and she took it out and it flew. She says
they think the window is the sky on a fair
day, she feeds birds too but hasn't got
so many. She says to hang strips of aluminum foil
in the window so we'll do that. She raved about
our birds. P.S. The book just come in the mail.

5.
Say, that book is sure good, I study
in it every day and enjoy our birds.
Some of them I can't identify
for sure, I guess they're females, the Latin words
I just skip over. Bet you'd never guess
the sparrows I've got here, House Sparrows you wrote,
but I have Fox Sparrows, Song Sparrows, Vesper Sparrows,
Pine Woods and Tree and Chipping and White Throat
and White Crowned Sparrows. I have six Cardinals,
three pairs, they come at early morning and night,
the males at the feeder and on the ground the females.
Juncos, maybe 25, they fight
for the ground, that's what they used to call snowbirds. I
          miss
the Bluebirds since the weather warmed. Their breast
is the color of a good ripe muskmelon. Tufted Titmouse
is sort of blue with a little tiny crest.
And I have Flicker and Red-Bellied and Red-
Headed Woodpeckers, you would die laughing
to see Red-Bellied, he hangs on with his head
flat on the board, his tail braced up under, wing
out. And Dickcissel and Ruby Crowned Ringlet
and Nuthatch stands on his head and Veery on top
the color of a bird dog and Hermit Thrush with spot

on breast, Blue Jay so funny, he will hop
right on the backs of the other birds to get the grain.
We bought some sunflower seeds just for him.
And Purple Finch I bet you never seen,
color of a watermelon, sits on the rim
of the feeder with his streaky wife, and the squirrels,
you know, they are cute too, they sit tall
and eat with their little hands, they eat bucketfuls.
I pulled my own tooth, it didn't bleed at all.

6.
It's sure a surprise how well Mother is doing,
she forgets her laxative but bowels move fine.
Now that windows are open she says our birds sing
all day. The girl took a Book of Knowledge on loan
from the library and I am reading up
on the habits of birds, did you know some males have
                three
wives, some migrate some don't. I am going to keep
feeding all spring, maybe summer, you can see
they expect it. Will need thistle seed for Goldfinch and
                Pine
Siskin next winter. Some folks are going to come see us
from Church, some bird watchers, pretty soon.
They have birds in town but nothing to equal this.

So the world woos its children back for an evening kiss.

Ellen Bryant Voigt

Short Story

My grandfather killed a mule with a hammer,
or maybe with a plank, or a stick, maybe
it was a horse — the story varied
in the telling. If he was planting corn
when it happened, it was a mule, and he was plowing
the upper slope, west of the house, his overalls
stiff to the knees with red dirt, the lines
draped behind his neck.
He must have been glad to rest
when the mule first stopped mid-furrow;
looked back at where he'd come, then down
to the brush along the creek he meant to clear.
No doubt he noticed the hawk's great leisure
over the field, the crows lumped
in the biggest elm on the opposite hill.
After he'd wiped his hatbrim with his sleeve,
he called to the mule as he slapped the line
along its rump, clicked and whistled.

My grandfather was a slight, quiet man,
smaller than most women, smaller
than his wife. Had she been in the yard,
seen him heading toward the pump now,
she'd pump for him a dipper of cold water.
Walking back to the field, past the corncrib,
he took an ear of corn to start the mule,
but the mule was planted. He never cursed
or shouted, only whipped it, the mule
rippling its backside each time

the switch fell, and when that didn't work
whipped it low on its side, where it's tender,
then cross-hatched the welts he'd made already.
The mule went down on one knee,
and that was when he reached for the blown limb,
or walked to the pile of seasoning lumber; or else,
unhooked the plow and took his own time to the shed
to get the hammer.
               By the time I was born,
he couldn't even lift a stick. He lived
another fifteen years in a chair,
but now he's dead, and so is his son,
who never meant to speak a word against him,
and whom I never asked what his father
was planting and in which field,
and whether it happened before he had married,
before his children came in quick succession,
before his wife died of the last one.
And only a few of us are left
who ever heard that story.

Visiting the Graves

All day we travel from bed to bed, our children
clutching home-made bouquets
of tulips and jonquils, hyacinth,
handfuls of yellow salad from the fields.
In Pittsylvania County, our dead face east,
my great-grandfather and his sons facing
what is now a stranger's farm.
One great-uncle chose a separate hill,
an absence in the only photograph.
Under the big oak, we fumble for his name
and the names of sisters scattered like coins.
But here is my father, near the stone
we watched him weep beside for twenty years.
And my mother beside him, the greenest slab of grass.
By horse, it was hours to Franklin County,
to Liberty Christian Church where her mother lies.
The children squabble in the car, roll on the velvet
slope of the churchyard, pout or laugh as we point out
the gap in the mountain where *her* mother's grave
is underwater, the lake lapping the house, the house
still standing like a tooth. We tell them how
we picked huckleberries from the yard,
tell them what a huckleberry is, but the oldest
can't keep straight who's still alive, the smallest
wants her flowers back—who can blame them,
this far from home, tired of trying
to climb a tree of bones. They fall asleep
halfway down the road, and we fall silent, too,
who were taught to remember and return,
my sister is driving, I'm in the back,
the sky before us a broken field of cloud.

A Marriage Poem

1.

Morning: the caged baby
sustains his fragile sleep.
The house is a husk against weather.
Nothing stirs — inside, outside.
With the leaves fallen,
the tree makes a web on the window
and through it
the world lacks color or texture,
like stones in the pasture
seen from this distance.

This is what is done with pain:
ice on the wound,
the isolating tourniquet —
as though to check an open vein
where the self pumps out of the self
would stop the second movement of the heart,
diastolic, inclusive:
to love is to siphon loss into that chamber.

2.

What does it mean when a woman says,
"my husband,"
if she sits all day in the tub;
if she worries her life like a dog a rat;
if her husband seems familiar but abstract,
a bandaged hand she's forgotten how to use.

They've reached the middle years.
Spared grief, they are given dread

as they tend the frail on either side of them.
Even their marriage is another child,
grown rude and querulous
since death practiced on them and withdrew.
He asks of her only a little lie,
a pale copy drawn from the inked stone
where they loll beside the unicorn,
great lovers then, two strangers
joined by appetite:

                     It frightens her,
to live by memory's poor diminished light.
She wants something crisp and permanent,
like coral — a crown, a trellis,
an iron shawl across the bed
where they are laced together,
the moon bleaching the house,
their bodies abandoned —

3.

In last week's mail,   .
still spread on the kitchen table,
the list of endangered species.
How plain the animals are,
quaint, domestic,
but the names lift from the page:
Woundfin. Whooping Crane. Squawfish.
Black-footed Ferret. California Least Tern.

Dearest, the beast of Loch Ness, that shy,
broad-backed, two-headed creature,
may be a pair of whales or manatee,
male and female,
driven from their deep mud nest,
who cling to each other,
circling the surface of the lake.

John Wieners

There Are So Many
Fatherless Children Around

"I never could stand you too long,
                don't you know,"
        a definite blockage
                concrete application.
The Graces are three Negro
                bims walking down Columbus Ave.
        or a woman's laughter from
                Shaker Heights or Santa Barbara.
        He never could forgive himself,
                for his father wanting to leave him.
He thought there was something wrong with him physically,
                so his cock turned to the left,
        did not know that was something between his man and wife
                took it upon himself imaginatively
                        to compensate for the loss.

Richard Wilbur

The Ride

The horse beneath me seemed
To know what course to steer
Through the horror of snow I dreamed,
And so I had no fear,

Nor was I chilled to death
By the wind's white shudders, thanks
To the veils of his patient breath
And the mist of sweat from his flanks.

It seemed that all night through,
Within my hand no rein
And nothing in my view
But the pillar of his mane,

I rode with magic ease
At a quick, unstumbling trot
Through shattering vacancies
On into what was not,

Till the weave of the storm grew thin,
With a threading of cedar-smoke,
And the ice-blind pane of an inn
Shimmered, and I awoke.

How shall I now get back
To the inn-yard where he stands,
Burdened with every lack,
And waken the stable-hands

To give him, before I think
That there was no horse at all,
Some hay, some water to drink,
A blanket and a stall?

4 / 5 / 74

The air was soft, the ground still cold.
In the dull pasture where I strolled
Was something I could not believe.
Dead grass appeared to slide and heave,
Though still too frozen-flat to stir,
And rocks to twitch, and all to blur.
What was this rippling of the land?
Was matter getting out of hand
And making free with natural law?
I stopped and blinked, and then I saw
A fact as eerie as a dream.
There was a subtle flood of steam
Moving upon the face of things.
It came from standing pools and springs
And what of snow was still around;
It came of winter's giving ground
So that the freeze was coming out,
As when a set mind, blessed by doubt,
Relaxes into mother-wit.
Flowers, I said, will come of it.

Alan Williamson

Friends Who Have Failed

They leave from positions of strength, like all baroque
civilizations; leave the statues we cannot imagine moving
for heaviness caught in the skirts . . .
We watch their gestures grow finer and more nervous
in the widening air.
They are the best judges of wine; talk always at the
                    glittering edges
of things, the terrible auras . . . The afternoons in their
                    houses
hang upside down, like objects seen through wine.
Their footfalls die an inch away in the carpet.

And leaving, we wonder why the world
has not appreciated this fineness; why clumsier juggling
finds favor in its slow eye . . .
But we have not understood the world; how its way
is to destroy without destroying, the way air
levels a mountain; things fly apart in a vacuum . . .
It wears us to the hard thing we cannot help being;
and if the only hard thing is our determination
not to be hard, it wears us down to that.

Robert Lowell: His Death

We will not find you by going back to London,
not even in another
heat-wave of the century, the fire-bells ringing
peacefully in the empty buildings all day Sunday. . .

or the floor-through room above Earl's Court, already
otherworldly: two or three chairs; worm-eaten dark
scrollwork around the Jacobean mirror;

the chest with a thousand snapshots drifted
inches-deep in the drawers — where, at a question, how
a house looked, a friend, your hand went hovering,
    looking —

* * *

Yet I cannot help imagining death
as one of your triumphs — down from the high air
where what you loved and feared stood: life
drawn up beside you,
                    Dante
equal in height to Purgatory, *the maker*
can't lift his painted hand to stop the crash

— for how often you wrote this, like many great men,
    unknowing —

With us no husband could sit out the marriage. . .
But you hung between two, and between two continents,
never
quite having to choose — the triumph — arriving dead
at your last true, though still divorced, wife's door;

without a reckoning; almost outside destiny. . .

*What shall I do with my stormy life blown towards
   evening?*

— Yet did not die in the air, but touched the earth
an instant — half a lifetime's goal — desiring
to do what others did, without afterthought; the senseless
detail: walked to the taxi line, with your bags

spoke to the driver, something
weightless about the weather;
slept; weren't there —

* * *

And the photographs you loved unmounted
at sea in the drawers of your only chest.

Anne Winters

The Key To The City

All middle age invisible to us, all age
passed close enough behind to seize our napehairs
and whisper in a voice all thatch and smoke
some village elder warning, some rasped-out
Remember me . . . Mute and grey in her city
uniform (stitch-lettered JUVENILE), the matron
just pointed me to a locker, and went out.
'What an old bag!' 'Got a butt on you, honey?' 'Listen,

did I get lost with these streetnames! Spruce
Street, Water, or get this, VANderwater—' Cautiously,
    coolly,
we lit up, crooking palms for the ashes. All fifteen
or under, all from Manhattan, we loitered bare
to the waist for the X-rays. In the whorling light
from one rainy window, our shapes were mere
outlines from floor to wall, opaque
as plaster, white, or terra-cotta, black . . .

'Names or numbers,' a skinny white girl with paleblue
    eyes
shrugged her shoulders. 'Why come here at all? You think
    little Susan
(thumb mockingly hooked at herself) needs working papers
to work in my uncle's diner? If they'd let me off school
at noon now — that's where the real tips are!'
And she smiled at our objections around her smoking
cigarette (I thought) like some museum mummy,
amber-fingered, fishhook collar bones—

'What are you talking? Don't you know the city
keeps like an eye we don't get overworked?'
'Yeah, and your Social Security number, that's
for life, girl, that ain't worth something to you?'
The skinny girl just cackled, goosepimpled arms
huddled against her ribs. 'Whadda you two, work
for the mayor? What's this (swinging her locker key
with its scarred wooden number) — the key to the city?'

She meant last week, when they'd offered it
to some visiting queen. Even I snickered. I
was younger than most of them, homesick among the
        near-
women's breasts and hair, even the familiar
girls' cloakroom odors: perspiration, powder, decades
of menstrual fust — 'Well I'm coming back in six
        months.'
This was one of the black girls, elbow swivelled
on pelvic sidethrust, fine hair-

filaments, finerimmed, sulky mouth. 'She'll be
sixteen, getting married,' the girl next over
burst in eagerly, 'He got a store job, still her folks
against it, they say stay in school. But every
afternoon—' Distantly, the first girl listened to
her own story, only breaking in at the end: 'I want a real
church wedding. Down here is just for the license, see?'
'A license,' said ''little Susan,'' sourly, 'like for a job?'

'His name is Harold Curtis,' was all she answered, then 'It
        too strong
for my parents. They see it too strong for them in the
        end.'
In our silence, the gutter slurred strangely. And for just
        one

moment, everyone breathless, the atmosphere grew
almost tender. But nobody knew what to say
except *good luck,* so we all went on smoking like chimneys
except the one murmur, of old and incurable
anger, 'Listen. Listen. They get you coming and going.'

Now each girl tilts her face down, contemplating
her own unseen choices, real
tips, the solitary and common
square foot of imaginary chance . . . Outside, the rain
was letting up. The city, like a graph
of its own mountainous causes, climbed in a mist
across our window. And then the matron came, calling
our locker numbers, one by one, for the X-rays.

'Jesus, it's late.' 'Hey honey, *I'm* ready!' 'Where'd we
      change
at from the D-Train?' Through the clearing air on the far
side of City Hall Park, I could see a narrow street
and a streetsign: Broadway. Miles to the north
my street had a number, and Broadway was really broad.
In the concrete prows of islands, the innumerable old
      women
were sitting, lonely as soldiers, silent as . . .
'What's up, girl? Goose step on your grave?'

Another number. And now, the room darker, each girl
cast about for the cheering word, when 'Listen,' I suddenly
heard my own voice saying, 'Guess what I saw coming
      down? A street
called Anne Street.'—'So what?'—'So my name is Anne.'
A pause, then 'Hey kid, that's really funny!' They all
grinned, and one of the older girls gave my shoulder
a tolerant punch. I was one of the youngest, and as far
as I can remember, that was all that I said.

David Wojahn

Dark-House Spearing

In my father's red sweater
I wake to snow in the South.
His first vacation alone,
he's sleeping on my sofa,

says again we never had a yellow Olds.
But I remember him
in his only suit,
leaving for his doctors in St. Paul,

1956, pushing snow from the wheels
of the yellow car:
the memory
from which I date the world.

We have learned the balm
of trivial disagreement,
though he doesn't believe in words.
We eat breakfast

at a restaurant window,
the river murky with ice.
Because his brother,
ten years younger, died last month

in alcoholic coma,
he doesn't want talk, just company.
But even here we mention snow,
the absence of color

from the interplay
of many colors.
He tells me I will never understand
the real simplicity of things.

                    *

So I remember dark-house spearing.
Christmas in the 50s,
we walked acros the bay
at Lake Millacs,

the flashlight glowing
by the circle we cut.
Fish swim curious,
illegal toward the light.

Dozens come. I'm five.
Father raises his grandfather's spear.
Sunfish and smallmouth swarm like bees.
Dark-house spearing,

Minnesota's sheer
December ice-mist around us.
I tell him how I woke
from the dream again last night,

of fish alive and trembling in the bag
I clutch riding home on his shoulders.
Sunrise. My uncle stands
at the window of my childhood home

and father and I are singing,
floating toward the light.
Useless to remember that, he says,
when you have the details wrong.

                    *

I have the details wrong.
Father, I wanted to evoke for you
words beyond the emptiness of words
so wholly it would be enough

to cause us to begin again.
Weeping, you told me
you could not remember
your last words with my uncle.

Daily, father, I wait
for the real simplicity of things.
Sometimes, when I shut my eyes
I'm back in ashen fields,

steel-colored sky.
My hands cling to the cedar fence
you said would hold
the world back from snow.

1956, I know already
snow will win, swirl in the livingrooms,
all night drift
against the beds and windows.

And those who rise at dawn,
rubbing the night from they eyes,
none of them will understand
what they wake to or have lost.

Charles Wright

Sex

The Holston lolls like a tongue here, its banks
Gummy and ill at ease; across the state line,
Moccasin Gap declines in a leafy sneer.
Darkness, the old voyeur, moistens his chapped lips.

Unnoticed by you, of course, your mind
Elsewhere and groping: *the stuck clasp, her knees,*
The circle around the moon, O anything...
— Black boat you step from, the wet's slow sift.

Then Nothing, sleek fish, nuzzles the surface calm.
The fireflies drag and relight.
The wound is unwound, the flash is tipped on the fuse,
And the long, long waters of What's Left.*

Franz Wright

There

Let it start to rain,
the streets are empty now.
Over the roof hear the leaves
coldly conversing in whispers;
a page turns in the book
left open by the window.
The streets are empty, now
it can begin. I am not there.

Like you
I wasn't present
at the burial. This morning

I have walked out
for the first time
and wander here
among the blind
flock of names
standing still
in the rain —

(the one on your stone
will remain
listed in the telephone books
for a long time, I guess, light
from a disappeared star. . .)

—just to locate the place,
to come closer, without knowing where you are
or if you know I am there.

Oberlin